# CONTENTS

I. **NUTRITION** . . . . . . . . . . . . . . . . . . . . . . . . . . . . . . . 2

    **Nutrients** . . . . . . . . . . . . . . . . . . . . . . . . . . . . . 2

    **MyPlate** . . . . . . . . . . . . . . . . . . . . . . . . . . . . . 10

    **Heart Healthy Eating and Special Diets** . . . . . . . . . . . . . 15

II. **FOOD PREPARATION** . . . . . . . . . . . . . . . . . . . . . 20

    **Cooking** . . . . . . . . . . . . . . . . . . . . . . . . . . . . . 20

    **Baking** . . . . . . . . . . . . . . . . . . . . . . . . . . . . . . 39

III. **MEAL PLANNING** . . . . . . . . . . . . . . . . . . . . . . . . 51

    **Menus** . . . . . . . . . . . . . . . . . . . . . . . . . . . . . . 51

    **Making a Grocery List** . . . . . . . . . . . . . . . . . . . . . 55

IV. **FOOD SERVICE** . . . . . . . . . . . . . . . . . . . . . . . . . 58

    **Styles of Table Service** . . . . . . . . . . . . . . . . . . . . . 58

    **Table Setting** . . . . . . . . . . . . . . . . . . . . . . . . . . 60

    **Table Waiting** . . . . . . . . . . . . . . . . . . . . . . . . . . 62

    **Glossary** . . . . . . . . . . . . . . . . . . . . . . . . . . . . . 68

    **Bibliography** . . . . . . . . . . . . . . . . . . . . . . . . . . . 69

Author:                              Marcia Parker, M.Ed.

Contributing Author:        Marcia A. Horan, B.S.

Editor:                             Alan Christopherson, M.S.

Illustrations:                    Alpha Omega Graphics

Alpha Omega Publications®

804 N. 2nd Ave. E., Rock Rapids, IA 51246-1759

# LET'S EAT

Making sure you get the right amount of nutrients every day will help you feel better and in turn look better. By eating a variety of foods, you will get the right amount of necessary nutrients that will help your body grow, develop, and work properly. Select foods from MyPlate throughout the day to make sure you get the right amounts of nutrients. This LIFEPAC® will explain good nutrition, how to select nutritious foods, and how to cope with special diet needs. Sitting down to a glorious meal with friends takes much planning and preparation.

This LIFEPAC will teach you to plan menus, buy groceries, and prepare that scrumptious meal as well as how to set the table and serve your guests. Have fun with the many hands-on projects you are about to experience.

## OBJECTIVES

**Read these objectives.** The objectives tell you what you will be able to do when you have successfully completed this LIFEPAC.

When you have completed this LIFEPAC, you should be able to:

1. Explain proper nutrition.

2. Identify the six main nutrients, their sources, and their uses by the body.

3. Identify the groups in MyPlate.

4. Understand the Dietary Guidelines for Americans.

5. Identify special dietary needs.

6. Demonstrate different techniques in food preparation.

7. Demonstrate skill in preparing various food items.

8. Demonstrate skill in planning menus.

9. Demonstrate skill in making a grocery list and purchasing the groceries.

10. Identify the different types and styles of table service.

11. Demonstrate skill in table setting and table waiting.

# I. NUTRITION

Nutrition is the result of the processes your body follows to use the food you eat. When you eat food to keep your body working properly, you are practicing good nutrition. What you eat now not only affects how you feel and look today, it also affects your future health. Your body and mind are growing at a rapid rate. Eating the proper foods will help you develop to the fullest extent possible.

The right amount of nutrients such as carbohydrates, fats, vitamins, minerals, protein, and water can improve the way you look and feel. Some nutrients affect your skin and hair, while others affect teeth and bones. An understanding of how to select the right foods from MyPlate will help you maintain the balance of nutrients that your body needs.

Learning to prepare for special diet needs will make you a more versatile cook who will be able to meet the nutritional needs of others. It should help you to strive to improve your eating habits now to avoid some of the diseases and health problems that develop later in life because of poor eating habits.

## SECTION OBJECTIVES

**Review these objectives.** When you have completed this section, you should be able to:

1.   Explain proper nutrition.

2.   Identify the six main nutrients, their sources, and their uses by the body.

3.   Identify the groups in MyPlate.

4.   Understand the Dietary Guidelines for Americans.

5.   Identify special dietary needs.

## NUTRIENTS

Food performs three essential services in the body: heat and energy, building and repairing body tissues and regulation of body processes. Nutrients are the chemical substances in food that are used by your body to keep it going. Six different nutrients are needed to keep your body healthy. They are proteins, carbohydrates, fats, vitamins, minerals, and water. People differ in the amounts of nutrients needed. We all need different amounts of energy. Traits that determine your daily requirements are your size, your age, your sex, your spiritual tone or emotions, the amount of activity you participate in and your **metabolism**. A balanced diet gives you enough nutrients and energy for you as a unique individual. The principle of individuality from LIFEPAC 1 states that we are made in the image of God but have our own unique qualities and needs. Therefore, although we all need the essential nutrients to stay healthy, our dietary needs and amounts of each nutrient may be different.

Nutrients work together in teams. All the team members must be there at the same time and in the right amounts. An extra amount of one nutrient can't make up for the lack of another. Your body needs about forty nutrients to keep it healthy. Nutrients are chemicals that build and repair body tissues. Each nutrient has a special use in the body.

Let's look at the six main nutrients, their sources and what they do for our bodies.

---

**NOTE:** Student, you should refer to the vocabulary words used in LIFEPAC 2: Mixing Terms, Cooking Terms, and the Glossary, throughout this LIFEPAC where needed.

complete proteins

incomplete proteins

## PROTEIN

Much of your body is made up of protein. Protein is used to build and repair tissues, to promote growth, to furnish heat and energy, and to assist in regulating body processes. Protein helps your body fight infections as well.

Protein is made up of smaller building blocks called amino acids. Complete proteins contain all the amino acids necessary to make body tissue. Sources of complete proteins are meat, eggs, and milk. Incomplete proteins are lacking in one or more essential amino acids. Plant products are incomplete proteins. These include fruits, vegetables, and grains. When you eat incomplete proteins you must put two or more together to get complete protein nutrition. Eating combination foods such as macaroni and cheese or a peanut butter sandwich on whole wheat bread will give you all the protein you need.

## CARBOHYDRATES

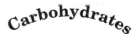

Carbohydrates

Carbohydrates are the best source of energy. They provide the body with most of the energy it needs. Your brain, nerves, and muscles must have carbohydrates in order to work properly. Starch, sugar, and fiber are carbohydrates. Simple carbohydrates such as sugar can be used by your body for quick energy. They provide calories but few other nutrients. Sugars are found in fruit and vegetables. Candy, soft drinks, and desserts are high in sugar, as well. Sugar is also added to many foods such as catsup, peanut butter, and cereal.

Complex Carbohydrates

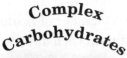

Starches are the main source of carbohydrates in the diet. Starches are complex carbohydrates. Complex carbohydrates are digested much more slowly than sugars. Whole grains and vegetables are high in complex carbohydrates. Legumes such as peas, beans, and seeds are high in complex carbohydrates. Bread, rice, and pasta are very good sources, too. Complex carbohydrates give us calories for energy. The amount of carbohydrates needed each day depends on a person's activities. Eating more carbohydrates than you need can cause weight gain. This is because your body stores starch and sugar that you do not need for energy as fat. If you do not eat enough carbohydrates you may feel tired.

**Thin person + too many carbohydrates = overweight person asleep on the couch.**

**Thin person + proper amount of carbohydrates = person exercising.**

Fiber is found in carbohydrates. Most fiber is complex carbohydrates. Fiber is a plant material that humans cannot digest. Fiber helps to regulate the bowel by helping to digest (break down) the food and get rid of body wastes. It helps prevent **constipation**. Fiber is found in fruits, vegetables, and grains.

## FATS

Your body needs fats in order to stay healthy and alive. Fats help your body use Vitamins A, D, E, and K. They also give your body energy. Your body needs some fat for the growth and development of healthy tissues. Fats also keep your skin from drying out. You need to eat only a small amount of fat each day. Fatty foods are high in calories. A teaspoon of fat has more than twice the calories than a teaspoon of sugar.

> **one teaspoon of butter vs one teaspoon sugar**
> **33 calories vs 15 calories!**

There are two kinds of fat. Saturated fats are usually solid at room temperature. Most come from animal fat such as meat, butter, cream, and milk. Polyunsaturated fats are usually oils. They are found in fish and most vegetable oils.

**WATER**

You can live longer without food than you can without water. Too little water causes kidney damage. Water helps your body by getting rid of waste. It helps control body temperature. Blood is made up of mostly water; it helps move nutrients around. You should drink at least eight glasses of water each day.

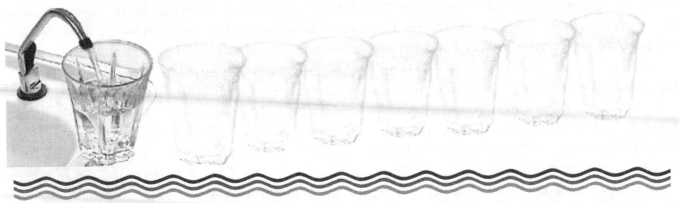

**Answer the following questions.**

1.1 Name the six nutrients.

a. _____

b. _____

c. _____

d. _____

e. _____

f. _____

1.2 Are complete proteins found in animal foods or plant foods? _____

1.3 Which nutrient is the best source of energy?_____

1.4 Plant proteins are _____ proteins.

1.5 Which nutrient is best used to build and repair tissues?_____

1.6 _____ help your body use vitamins A, D, E, and K.

1.7 _____ is a complex carbohydrate that helps regulate the bowel.

1.8 Your body stores _____ to use for energy later.

1.9 The amount of carbohydrates needed each day depends on a person's _____ .

1.10 Foods such as pasta are a good source of _____ .

*True* **or** *False.*

1.11 _____ Starch is bad for you.

1.12 _____ Sugar is higher in calories than fat.

1.13 _____ Too little water can cause kidney damage.

1.14 _____ Good nutrition means eating a healthy diet.

1.15 _____ Vegetables contain complex carbohydrates.

5

## VITAMINS

Vitamins are substances needed by the body for growth and maintenance. Vitamins also help regulate the chemical processes in your body. They help your body store and use energy for growth and development. Although required in very small amounts, vitamins are essential to life and health.

Vitamins are found in tiny amounts in food. Vitamins that cannot be stored by the body are called water soluble vitamins. Vitamin C and the B vitamins are water soluble; they dissolve in water. You cannot get too many of these vitamins and any excess taken in is lost in the urine.

Vitamin C (Ascorbic Acid) is necessary to the health of every cell in the body, especially the blood vessels. It helps produce a substance that holds body cells together. It helps broken bones mend and wounds to heal. It helps you to resist infection and helps maintain healthy skin, gums, and teeth. Since Vitamin C is water soluble and not stored in the body, you should eat foods rich in Vitamin C each day.

**Vitamin C**

Vitamin C is found in many fruits and vegetables. Citrus fruits such as oranges and grapefruit are great sources as well as cantaloupe, strawberries, broccoli, and tomatoes.

The B vitamins are a group of vitamins that work together in your body. Three key B vitamins are thiamin ($B_1$), riboflavin ($B_2$), and niacin ($B_3$). These vitamins promote growth, good appetite, and proper digestion. They help keep your nervous system healthy and prevent irritability. They also keep your skin healthy.

**Vitamin B**

Like Vitamin C, the B vitamins are water soluble so you need to include them in your diet every day. Sources of B vitamins are plentiful. Foods that are rich in B vitamins are whole grains and enriched breads and cereals. Leafy green vegetables, legumes, meat, milk, and eggs are also good sources.

**Fill in the blanks.**

1.16    Vitamins are substances that are needed by the body for _____ and maintenance.

1.17    Vitamins that _____ are water soluble.

**Write *C* in front of the phrase that tells something about Vitamin C and write *B* in front of the phrase that tells something about the B vitamins.**

1.18    _____    helps keep teeth and gums healthy

1.19    _____    is found in meat and whole grains

1.20    _____    is found in citrus fruits

1.21    _____    helps resist infection

1.22    _____    helps promote proper digestion

Other vitamins can be stored by the body and are called fat-soluble vitamins. They are Vitamins A, D, E, and K. Vitamin pills which contain high levels of fat-soluble vitamins are harmful. Your body cannot get rid of the extra amounts. It is better to get these vitamins from the foods that you eat. Each vitamin has a special function in the body. Each is needed for good health.

Vitamin A is necessary for healthy skin and mucous membranes, sound teeth, strong bones, and growth. It is important for vision, especially night vision.

Your body can make Vitamin A from carotene. **Carotene** is found in dark green and yellow vegetables: spinach, winter squash, carrots, sweet potatoes, cantaloupe, and apricots. You can also get some ready made Vitamin A in animal foods like liver, eggs, butter, and cream.

Vitamin D helps your body use the minerals needed for strong bones and teeth. This function is especially important when your body is growing and developing. Vitamin D is sometimes called the "sunshine" vitamin because your body can make Vitamin D when exposed to sunlight. Fortified milk is a good source of Vitamin D. Cod liver oil and other fish are sources of Vitamin D, too.

Vitamin E is believed to keep the oxygen in the body from destroying nutrients, especially Vitamin A. So many foods contain Vitamin E that people rarely suffer from deficiencies. Some important sources are vegetable oils, whole grain breads and cereals, eggs, organ meats, and green leafy vegetables.

Vitamin K helps to clot the blood. Many foods contain Vitamin K so deficiencies are rare. Some important sources are green leafy vegetables, cauliflower, liver, and eggs.

**Answer the following questions.**

1.23 Vitamins that can be stored by the body are called _____ .

1.24 Vitamin _____ is important for vision and is found in dark _____ and _____ vegetables.

1.25 Vitamin _____ is the "sunshine" vitamin.

1.26 Vitamin D is important for strong _____ and _____ .

1.27 What is a good food source of Vitamin D? _____

1.28 Which vitamin helps the oxygen in the body from destroying nutrients? _____

1.29 What is the primary function of Vitamin K? _____

## MINERALS

Minerals are another kind of nutrient needed for a healthy body. Minerals help to regulate many of your body's activities. They help muscles contract and nerves transmit signals to and from the brain. They also help maintain the body's water balance and build strong blood, bones, and teeth.

Although there are many needed minerals, the most important are calcium, phosphorous, chlorine, potassium, and sodium. Also included are the trace minerals: iron, iodine, and fluorine. Trace minerals are minerals that are found only in small amounts in the body.

Calcium and phosphorous are two minerals that work together as a team. Both are more effective when the other is present. They are both needed for strong bones and teeth. They are important for clotting of the blood and for normal heart and muscle formation.

The richest sources of calcium are milk and milk products including yogurt and hard cheeses. Other good sources are fish and green leafy vegetables. Foods that are rich in calcium are also rich in phosphorous.

Sodium, chlorine, and potassium work together as a team in your body. They help keep the right amount of fluid around and inside of the cells in your body. They allow the cells to take up the nutrients from the blood. These minerals also help the nerves and muscles function as they should.

These minerals are found in many foods. Sodium and chlorine are found in table salt. Bananas, orange juice, green leafy vegetables, and milk are all good sources of potassium.

Iron is a trace mineral that is extremely important for the development of healthy red blood cells. Lack of iron can cause **anemia**. Symptoms of anemia are a tired feeling, lack of energy, and a loss of appetite.

Liver is an excellent source of iron. Other sources are meat, fish, nuts, eggs, dried beans and peas, and whole grain or enriched breads and cereals.

---

**Especially for Girls:** Eating enough foods that contain iron is especially important to females because they lose iron during their monthly menstrual cycle.

---

Iodine is used to help the thyroid gland produce a hormone that affects growth and weight. If your body does not receive enough iodine, the thyroid can grow larger because it is trying to produce this hormone. This condition is called a **goiter** which is a swelling in the front of the throat.

Iodized salt contains iodine. Most people use enough salt to meet their needs for this mineral. Salt water fish are also a good source of iodine.

Fluorine, in the form of fluoride, is needed for the development of strong bones and teeth. Fluorine is helpful in the prevention of tooth decay. It is added to many brands of toothpaste. Fluorine is often added to municipal drinking water. Small amounts are also found in meats, milk and eggs.

........................................................................

**Name the mineral or minerals important to the following.**

1.30 Bone growth _____

1.31 Functioning of red blood cells _____

1.32 Thyroid gland activity _____

1.33 Prevention of tooth decay _____

1.34   Prevention of anemia _____

1.35   Keeps the right amount of fluid around and inside the cells _____


**Fill in the blanks.**

1.36   List three good sources of calcium.

    a. _____

    b. _____

    c. _____

1.37   Name one food source of iodine. _____

1.38   Define the term *trace minerals*. _____

_____


**Complete the following activity.**

1.39   Fill in the following table as completely as you can for a study guide. Beside each nutrient in the chart, explain why the nutrient is needed by your body and name food sources of the nutrient.

| NUTRIENT | WHY NEEDED | SOURCES |
|---|---|---|
| Proteins | | |
| Carbohydrates | | |
| Fats | | |
| Vitamin A | | |
| B Vitamins | | |
| Vitamin C | | |
| Vitamin D | | |

9

| NUTRIENT | WHY NEEDED | SOURCES |
|---|---|---|
| Vitamin E | | |
| Vitamin K | | |
| Calcium and Phosphorous | | |
| Iron | | |
| Iodine | | |
| Fluorine | | |
| Sodium, Chlorine and Potassium | | |
| Water | | |

Adult Check _____

Initial          Date

## MYPLATE

For many years, Americans followed the United States Department of Agriculture (USDA) created Food Pyramid. In 2010 they created MyPlate.

The new food guide specifies food choices for the total diet because both nutrient adequacy and excesses are of concern. The specific nutrient levels targeted are the Recommended Dietary Allowances (RDAs) for protein, vitamins, minerals, and levels of food components such as oils, saturated fat, cholesterol, sodium, and fiber recommended by the Dietary Guidelines and by consensus reports of authoritative health organizations.

## DIETARY GUIDELINES FOR AMERICANS

- Eat a variety of foods.
- Balance the food you eat with physical activity—maintain or improve your weight.
- Choose a diet with plenty of grain products, vegetables, and fruit.
- Choose a diet that includes oils but is low in fat, saturated fat, and cholesterol.
- Choose a diet moderate in sugars.
- Choose a diet moderate in salt and sodium.
- Avoid alcoholic beverages.

MyPlate divides food into five basic groups. Oils are not a food group but they do provide some needed nutrients. Solid fats and sugars add calories to food but they have no nutrients. Since they do not provide nutrients they are called empty calories. MyPlate shows us how to choose healthy foods. It tells us how much of what foods we need. Learning which foods are in each group will help you choose foods that are good for you. Learning the number of servings you should have each day will help you get all the needed nutrients. In MyPlate, foods we should eat more often have a larger color and those we should eat less frequently are smaller. Everyone in the family can find more information about how to eat better and exercise more to stay healthy at the Web site, *MyPlate.gov.*

## Grains: 4–10 Servings

These foods provide you with complex carbohydrates, an important source of energy. They also provide B vitamins, minerals, and fiber. Choose whole grain foods to maximize fiber and other nutrients. Limit items high in fat and sugar such as cookies and cake. Starchy foods are not fattening if you don't add butter, cheese or cream sauces. Most teens need about six servings from this group each day.

1 serving:

    1 slice bread
    small roll or muffin
    1/2 of a bun, bagel or English muffin
    1 to 1 1/2 ounces ready-to-eat cereal
    1/2 cup cooked cereal, rice or pasta
    3 or 4 small or 2 large crackers
    2 breadsticks (4 1/2 inch)
    3 cups popcorn
    2 medium cookies

## Fruits: 2–4 Servings

The fruit group includes fresh, frozen, canned and dried fruits and fruit juices. Fruits are rich sources of vitamins, especially Vitamin C. They are low in fat and calories. Deep yellow orange fruits are high in Vitamin A. The fruits that have the most Vitamin C are citrus fruits, strawberries, and cantaloupe. Choose fresh fruits for the fiber. Read labels to be sure that you are drinking 100% fruit juice and not fruit drinks. Teens need three servings from this group each day.

1 serving:

    1 medium fresh fruit (apple, banana, orange, etc.) or 1/2 grapefruit
    1 medium wedge melon
    3/4 cup fruit juice
    1/2 cup berries
    1/2 cup cooked or canned fruit
    1/4 cup dried fruit

## Vegetables: 3–5 Servings

Vegetables provide vitamins (especially A and C), are excellent sources of fiber and are naturally low in fat. For maximum nutrients select dark leafy greens, deep-yellow or orange vegetables and starchy vegetables like potatoes and yams. Different vegetables provide different nutrients. Corn and potatoes provide starch. Broccoli and green peppers are good sources of Vitamin C. Carrots and squash are high in vitamin A. Dried beans and peas provide protein. Choose a variety of vegetables to get all the nutrients. Teens need four servings of this group each day.

1 serving:

    1/2 cup chopped raw, cooked or canned vegetables
    3/4 cup vegetable juice
    1 cup raw leafy vegetables
    1 medium potato

## Protein: 2–3 Servings

Animal foods are excellent sources of protein, iron, zinc, and B vitamins, as are beans, nuts and seeds. Tofu (made from soybeans) and white beans also supply calcium. Some seeds, like almonds, are good sources of Vitamin E. Choose lean meat and poultry without the skin to reduce fat. Eggs are high in cholesterol and nuts are high in fat. It is better to eat them occasionally. Fish and dried beans are good low fat choices. Teens also need 2–3 servings from this group.

1 serving:

2 to 3 ounces cooked lean meat, poultry or fish (3 ounces is about the size of an average hamburger or medium chicken breast half)

4 ounces tofu

Count the following as 1 ounce of meat:
   1 egg (maximum of 3 weekly)
   3 egg whites
   2 tablespoons peanut butter or whole nuts or seeds
   1/2 cup cooked dried beans

## Dairy: 2–3 Servings

Milk products are the richest sources of calcium. They also provide protein and Vitamin B$_{12}$. Choose low fat varieties to keep calories, cholesterol, and saturated fat at a minimum. Teens need three servings from this group each day.

1 serving:
   1 cup milk, yogurt, or pudding
   1 1/2 ounces cheese
   1 1/2 cups ice cream, ice milk or frozen yogurt
   2 cups cottage cheese

## Fats, Oils, and Sweets: Use Sparingly

These foods provide calories, but little else nutritionally. These foods include margarine, butter, cream, candy, soft drinks, and salad dressings. Exceptions are vegetable oil, which is a rich source of vitamin E (one tablespoon is all you need) and molasses, an excellent source of iron.

 **Fill in the blanks.**

1.40   List the seven Dietary Guidelines for Americans.

   a. _____

   b. _____

   c. _____

   d. _____

   e. _____

   f. _____

   g. _____

1.41    How does MyPlate differ from other food guides? _____

_____

1.42    The foods that we need the most are _____ on MyPlate.

**Fill in the following chart giving the food group, the number of servings needed by most adults, the recommended number of servings for teens and the nutrients gained by eating these foods.**

1.43

| FOOD GROUP | # OF SERVINGS FOR ADULTS | # OF SERVINGS FOR TEENS | NUTRIENT(S) |
|---|---|---|---|
| a. | | | |
| b. | | | |
| c. | | | |
| d. | | | |
| e. | | | |
| f.  Fats, Oils, Sweets | | | |

A balanced diet contains foods that will give you enough nutrients and energy. All people need about the same kinds of nutrients, but people differ in the amounts of nutrients needed. We all need different amounts of energy too. Your nutrient and energy needs change as you grow and mature.

Many things affect nutrition needs. Babies, children, and teens have high nutrient needs because they are growing. Women who are pregnant or are breast-feeding need more nutrients. People recovering from sickness need more nutrients than healthy people. Women need more iron than men, but men need more total nutrients because they are usually larger in stature and size than women.

The Dietary Guidelines and MyPlate are for Americans two years of age and older. Infants and toddlers have special dietary needs because of their rapid growth and development. Follow the advice of a health care provider in feeding them.

As young children begin to eat the same foods as the family, usually about the age of two years or older, offer them foods that are moderate in

**A balanced diet will give you enough energy.**

fat and saturated fat but provide the calories and nutrients they need for normal growth. Serve young children the same variety of foods as everyone else, but in smaller amounts to suit their smaller needs—about 2/3 of the adult serving size. Be sure they have at least the equivalent of two cups of milk each day. Because young children often eat only a small amount at one time, offer them nutritious "meal foods" as snacks.

Calorie needs vary widely for elementary school children. They should eat at least the lower number of servings from each of the five major food groups daily. Most children will need more calories for growth and activity; they should eat larger portions of food from the major food groups and some nutritious snacks. Calorie intake should be around 2,000 calories per day. Encourage physical activity.

Teenagers and young adults to age 24 should have three servings of milk, cheese, or yogurt daily to meet their calcium needs. Bone density increases well into the twenties. Eating foods providing adequate calcium to attain maximum bone density is very important in helping prevent **osteoporosis** and bone fractures later in life. Most teenage boys will need to eat the higher number of servings from each food group—2,800 calories. Most teenage girls will probably need about 2,200 calories and the middle of the ranges of servings especially when they are active or growing. Teenage girls who participate in vigorous sports may need the higher numbers of servings. To control weight, encourage physical activity rather than repeated dieting.

**Young women need plenty of calcium.**

The lower numbers of servings from each food group—1,600 calories is about right for **sedentary** women and some older adults. Other adults will need more calories than this, depending on body size and physical activity. Most men will need the middle to upper numbers of servings in the ranges. The lower to middle numbers of servings in the ranges are more appropriate for calorie needs of most women. Regular exercise is important for all adults to maintain fitness.

**Answer the following questions.**

1.44 People differ in the amounts of _____ and _____ needed.

1.45 List two things that affect nutrient needs.

   a. _____

   b. _____

1.46 At what age should a child begin using the Dietary Guideline of Americans and MyPlate?
   _____

1.47 A child's serving should be about _____ of the adult serving size.

1.48 Bone _____ increases well into the twenties, so drinking _____ servings of milk daily is important to teens.

## HEART HEALTHY EATING AND SPECIAL DIETS

Foods from MyPlate may be part of any meal. A grilled cheese sandwich or a bowl of whole-grain cereal is just as nutritious in the morning as it is at noon. A good breakfast consists of any foods that supply about one-fourth of the necessary nutrients for the day.

Just as wise shoppers get the most for their money, so wise eaters select foods that give the most nutrition for the lowest number of calories. For example, snacks can furnish about one-fourth of the calorie requirements among teenagers. Those snacks should also furnish one-fourth of the day's allowances for protein, minerals, and vitamins. Sandwiches, fruit, and milk make good snacks for active teenagers.

Fast foods and convenience foods are major parts of many people's diets. Convenience foods, such as TV dinners and cake mixes, are those prepared at home from foods already cooked or otherwise processed before reaching the retail store. Fast foods are prepared in quick-order restaurants.

A meal consisting of a cheeseburger with lettuce, tomato, and onion, French fries, and a milk shake, though high in fat and sodium, does include foods from each of the groups in MyPlate. So does a taco with its corn meal shell, ground beef, shredded cheese, lettuce, olives, and tomato.

Frequent fast-food meals, though, require some thought about nutrients and calories. High in protein, iron, and B vitamins, fast-food meals are sometimes low in calcium and Vitamins A and C and often extremely high in sodium. A milk shake provides calcium, but it can also be high in fat and contain more than 800 calories.

Depending on the items ordered, a typical fast-food meal ranges from 900 to 1,800 calories. A burger with all the trimmings has about 600 calories, but a plain cheeseburger has only about half as many calories and a plain hamburger even less. A serving of pizza can have from 300 to 600 or more calories.

Special diets for people with health problems should be prescribed by a physician. Many doctors refer patients to a **dietitian** who draws up individual diet plans.

The typical diet in the United States contains much more salt than the body needs. Persons with high blood pressure must avoid as much salt as possible. Diabetes mellitus is another disease that requires careful meal planning. In diabetes mellitus the body does not make normal use of glucose, or blood sugar. In addition to a special diet, diabetic children and some adults need medication (i.e., insulin). If diabetes develops later in life, it often can be controlled with diet alone.

Diets high in fat and cholesterol have been linked to blockage of the arteries, a common factor in heart disease and stroke. Studies show that this condition can begin in adolescence or earlier.

Cholesterol is a fat-like substance found in blood, tissues, and some food. Some body cholesterol is normal and helpful, but too much of a certain kind of cholesterol is harmful. Cholesterol is found only in foods from animals. Eggs, butter, cheese, meat, and shellfish are high in cholesterol. The body also produces cholesterol. Sometimes it makes too much. This can be a serious problem for some people.

Some people are vegetarians; that is, they eat no meat and sometimes no eggs, cheese, or milk. Those who avoid all animal products are called *vegans* (pronounced *vee-gans*). Such people must plan their diets carefully to have balanced meals, for they often lack protein.

Malnutrition is the imbalance between the body's demand for nutrients and the available supply of nutrients. Malnutrition can result from an unsatisfactory diet or from a disorder that interferes with the body's use of food.

Obesity, or the state of being excessively fat, is a form of malnutrition that contributes to many health problems. It may be defined as body weight more than 20 percent above a person's ideal weight.

Anorexia nervosa is a condition characterized by extreme weight loss. Nervosa means *of the nerves*, or *neurotic*. This life-threatening disease generally occurs in young women; however, some men are also susceptible. It requires treatment by professionals.

Protein-calorie malnutrition, known as *kwashiorkor*, is common among children in unindustrialized nations. A lack of protein results in failure of the body to grow and often damages digestive organs. A severe calorie deficiency results from starvation.

Mineral and vitamin deficiencies are responsible for various disorders. Insufficient iron can cause iron-deficiency anemia. Lack of iodine can cause goiter, an enlargement of the thyroid gland.

Vitamin A deficiency causes loss of vision in dim light (night vision). Vitamin D deficiency leads to a faulty deposit of calcium in bones and teeth, resulting in rickets. A child with rickets may have bowed legs and a prominent sternum (breastbone). Vitamin C deficiency is known as scurvy. It causes infected and bleeding gums and painful joints.

Vitamin $B_1$ deficiency, or beriberi, damages the nerves, heart, and circulation. Whole-grain flour and enriched flour that is processed in the United States contains Vitamin $B_1$.

Vitamin $B_{12}$ deficiency causes blood disorders and affects the nervous system. It rarely results from an inappropriate diet but usually from a defect of absorption in the digestive tract.

 **Answer the following questions.**

1.49   What percentage of daily nutrient requirements should breakfast provide? _____

1.50   Define *convenience foods*. _____

_____

1.51   Fast food meals are sometimes low in _____ and _____ and often are extremely high in _____ .

1.52   Persons with high blood pressure should avoid _____ .

1.53   In diabetes mellitus, the body does not make normal use of _____ , or blood sugar.

1.54   What nutrient might a vegan lack in his diet? _____

1.55   Define obesity. _____

1.56   Who is more likely to be diagnosed with anorexia nervosa? _____

1.57   Lack of iodine can cause _____ , an enlargement of the _____ .

1.58   A deficiency in the following can cause:

a.   Vitamin A   _____

b.   Vitamin D   _____

c.   Vitamin C   _____

d.   Vitamin $B_1$   _____

e.   Vitamin $B_{12}$   _____

Review the material in this section in preparation for the Self Test. The Self Test will check your mastery of this particular section. The items missed on this Self Test will indicate specific areas where restudy is needed for mastery.

# SELF TEST 1

**Match each word to its definition** (each answer, 2 points).

1.01 _____ chemicals or building blocks used to make proteins

1.02 _____ proteins that are low in one or more amino acids

1.03 _____ proteins with all the amino acids needed to make body tissues

1.04 _____ starches

1.05 _____ sugars

1.06 _____ nutrients best used to repair and build tissues

1.07 _____ a plant material that humans cannot digest

1.08 _____ a fat-like substance found in blood, tissues, and food

a. amino acids

b cholesterol

c. complete proteins

d. fiber

e. complex carbohydrates

f. incomplete proteins

g. simple carbohydrates

h. proteins

**List the six nutrients** (each answer, 3 points).

1.09 _____

1.010 _____

1.011 _____

1.012 _____

1.013 _____

1.014 _____

**Match the vitamin to its function or source.** Answers may be used more than once (each answer, 2 points).

1.015 _____ helps keep teeth and gums healthy

1.016 _____ is found in meat and whole grains

1.017 _____ important for vision

1.018 _____ helps clot the blood

1.019 _____ "sunshine" vitamin

1.020 _____ found in carrots

1.021 _____ helps promote proper digestion

a. Vitamin A

b. Vitamin B₁

c. Vitamin C

d. Vitamin D

e. Vitamin K

**Match the mineral to its function** (each answer, 2 points).

1.022 _____ prevention of tooth decay

1.023 _____ thyroid gland activity

1.024 _____ bone growth

1.025 _____ prevention of anemia

a. calcium

b. iron

c. iodine

d. fluoride

**Write the letter of the correct answer on each blank** (each answer, 3 points).

1.026 Teens need _____ servings each day from the grains group.
   a. 8  b. 6
   c. 10  d. 11

1.027 Fruit is the best source of _____ .
   a. fiber  b. carbohydrates
   c. sugar  d. vitamins

1.028 Broccoli and green peppers are a good source of _____ .
   a. Vitamin A  b. Vitamin B
   c. Vitamin C  d. Vitamin D

1.029 The best source of protein is _____ .
   a. vegetables  b. milk
   c. meat  d. fruit

1.030 The best source of calcium is _____ .
   a. vegetables  b. milk
   c. meat  d. fruit

1.031 Children should start using the Dietary Guidelines of Americans and MyPlate at the age of
   _____ .
   a. 9 months  b. 1 year
   c. 2 years  d. 3 years

**Matching** (each answer, 3 points).

1.032 _____ extreme weight loss

1.033 _____ imbalance between the body's demand for nutri-
         ents and the supply of nutrients to the body

1.034 _____ abnormal glucose level

1.035 _____ iron-deficiency

1.036 _____ Vitamin D deficiency

1.037 _____ body weight more the 20% above the ideal weight

1.038 _____ Vitamin A deficiency

1.039 _____ lack of iodine

1.040 _____ Vitamin C deficiency

a. malnutrition

b. obesity

c. anorexia nervosa

d. anemia

e. goiter

f. night blindness

g. scurvy

h. rickets

i. diabetes

81
101

Score _____

Adult Check _____
Initial          Date

19

# II. FOOD PREPARATION

Food is part of our recreation today. At home, at the ball park, at school, at the candy store, at the pizza place—wherever friends meet, a special kind of food helps make the fun. It is a challenge to have the food you need and not eat too many calories.

The notion of what makes "fun food" differs from home to home, as it does from country to country. If you dropped in on a Chinese teenager, you might be offered a bun filled with bean paste. New England's Indian pudding could seem strange to a Southerner more accustomed to black-eyed peas. Frosted layer cakes such as we take for granted would be grand-occasion productions in other parts of the world. Pizza was a local Italian specialty until a few generations ago.

You can add to your own food enjoyment by being willing to try other people's favorites. The best way to assure that you get all the foods you need is to enjoy the wide variety of types of food available to us—varied in color, in texture, in flavor, and even in the way in which they are prepared.

This section of the LIFEPAC will give you the opportunity to cook and bake from the food groups found in MyPlate.

## SECTION OBJECTIVES

**Review these objectives.** When you have completed this section, you should be able to:

6. Demonstrate different techniques in food preparation.

7. Demonstrate skill in preparing various food items.

## COOKING

**Cereals.** The most common grains used in cereals are wheat, oats, corn, and rice. Cereal can be classified into two groups: prepared (ready-to-eat cereals) and cooked cereals.

The prepared cereals which are nutritionally most desirable are those made from whole grains, but the others—the many delicious flakes and puffed grains and shreds—are valuable not only as a source of energy, but also because of the variety they bring into the diet.

Crispness is the most important characteristic of these cereals and they retain their crispness well until their air-tight seal is broken. They can be easily freshened, by spreading the cereal on a baking sheet and placing it in a slow oven for a few minutes. On cooling, it will become as fresh and crisp as ever.

Cooked cereals such as cream of wheat and oatmeal can be cooked and ready to serve in five to ten minutes (or only two when cooked in the microwave). Cooked cereals should be served hot. The flavor of cooked cereal can be enhanced by adding spices such as cinnamon, nutmeg or cocoa. Brown sugar on your hot cereal is more nutritious than white sugar and really tasty. You can also add raisins, honey, maple syrup, jellies, jams, and preserves as sweetener alternatives. Berries, bananas, and sliced peaches are favorite toppings for both prepared and cooked cereals.

**Rice and Pasta.** Rice and the spaghetti type of cereal food require very rapid cooking in a large amount of boiling water. They will swell from two to four times during cooking, so that 1/2 pound of rice, macaroni, spaghetti or noodles is usually sufficient for serving five persons. All of these foods should be dropped into boiling water slowly so that at no time does the water stop boiling.

Only rice needs to be rinsed before cooking. This is done to remove the loose starch with which it is coated. The rice should be washed with cold water several times until the water is clear, then drained thoroughly before cooking. If separate, fluffy rice is desired, then the rice should be rinsed after cooking by putting it in a colander and letting the water run through it. The colander should then be placed over boiling water, covered with a clean cloth and steamed until the grains are fluffy.

Precooked rice can be fixed in 5 to 10 minutes by following the directions on the box. It may lack in nutrition and taste, but it is easy and quick to fix for those busy days.

Spaghetti and macaroni also need rinsing after they are cooked if they are to be used in a dish such as Italian spaghetti or macaroni salad where it is important that the pieces do not stick together. If it is to be served hot, rinse with hot water; if it is to be chilled for salad, use cold water.

---

**Answer the following questions.**

2.1     What are the most common grains used in cereals? _____

2.2     Cereals can be classified into what two groups? _____

2.3     What is the most important characteristic of prepared cereals? _____

2.4     What are two of the most common cooked cereals? _____

2.5     How much pasta do you need to prepare for five people? _____ Why such a small amount?

_____

2.6     Why should you rinse rice before cooking? _____

2.7     What is the rule concerning when to rinse spaghetti and macaroni after is has been cooked?

_____

**Complete the following activity.**

2.8     Prepare a hot dish of oatmeal or cream of wheat on the stove, not in the microwave. Serve with a special topping of your choice.

•Note: Cereal should be hot and creamy, not lumpy, and have a rich flavor. It should be served with a special topping.

**Adult Check** _____

                    **Initial          Date**

**Vegetables.** Vegetables are classified according to how they grow. Study the chart below.

| TYPES OF VEGETABLES | | | | |
|---|---|---|---|---|
| **Root vegetables** | beets<br>onions | potatoes<br>sweet potatoes | carrots<br>parsnips | radishes |
| **Stem vegetables** | asparagus | celery | rhubarb | |
| **Flower vegetables** | artichokes | broccoli | cauliflower | |
| **Seed vegetables** | beans<br>cucumbers<br>okra | peas<br>pumpkin<br>tomatoes | corn<br>green beans | peppers<br>squash |
| **Leafy vegetables** | cabbage<br>collards<br>escarole | lettuce<br>romaine<br>watercress | chard<br>curly endive<br>kale | parsley<br>spinach<br>various greens |

No matter how they are prepared, from steamed to creamed, vegetables make your meal more complete and certainly more colorful. They are nutritious and one of today's best bargains at the grocery store.

Fresh is always best when serving vegetables plain. Lightly steamed they add a delectable crunchiness to your meal. Save money, however and use frozen or canned vegetables when you plan to combine them in a casserole, sauce or soups.

Some quick helpful hints for preparing vegetables:

1. Freeze fresh herbs in small quantities and add, still frozen, to any dish before it's cooked. (See Herbs and Spices Chart)
2. Green vegetables stay bright green if cooked uncovered. Adding a little lemon to the water will also help them stay green.
3. Rule of thumb for cooking vegetables: Vegetables grown underground: cook covered. Above ground vegetables: cook uncovered. (See Table of Vegetables above).
4. Remember, fresh vegetables stay fresh longer if stored in covered containers or plastic bags in the refrigerator.
5. If you double the vegetable recipe, increase the liquids, herbs, and spices by less than one-half.
6. Cooking vegetables in salted water tends to draw the vitamins out of the vegetables into the water. Add salt just before you serve. Cook vegetables in a minimum amount of water.
7. When you prepare creamed vegetables, use evaporated milk instead of fresh milk for a richer flavor in the cream sauce.
8. Heat canned vegetables only to the simmering point before serving.
9. Add leftover vegetables to the soup pot or freeze them for use in future soups.
10. Sautéing can be the most delicious way to cook vegetables, but not if you let them get mushy. Watch the pan closely.

# FLAVOR MAKERS...HERBS AND SPICES

| Spice/Herb | Meat/Dairy | Fish/Eggs/Poultry | Vegetables | Fruit | Breads/Sweets |
|---|---|---|---|---|---|
| **Allspice** | Ground beef<br>Ham<br>Roasts<br>Sausages<br>Stews | Clam chowder<br>Oysters | Beets<br>Red cabbage<br>Spinach<br>Sweet potatoes<br>Tomatoes | Apples<br>Bananas<br>Cherries<br>Citrus fruit<br>Peaches | Cookies<br>Fruit pies<br>Mincemeat<br>Pumpkin pie<br>Spice cake |
| **Basil** | Beef<br>Cheese dishes<br>Liver<br>Pork<br>Veal | Duck<br>Egg dishes<br>Goose<br>Seafood<br>Turkey | Carrots<br>Green beans<br>Peas<br>Summer squash<br>Tomatoes | | |
| **Celery (seed, salt, flakes)** | Cheese mixtures<br>Ham spread<br>Meat loaf<br>Roasts<br>Stews | Chicken<br>  casseroles<br>Chowders<br>Deviled eggs<br>Seafood | Coleslaw<br>Corn<br>Potatoes<br>Sauerkraut<br>Tomatoes | Fruit salads<br>Fruit salad<br>  dressings | Bread |
| **Cinnamon** | Ham<br>Lamb<br>Pork | Chicken<br>Duck<br>Fish | Artichokes<br>Beans<br>Beets<br>Carrots<br>Pumpkin<br>Sweet potatoes | Apples<br>Cranberries<br>Dates<br>Grapefruit<br>Peaches<br>Pineapple | Cakes<br>Cheesecake<br>Chocolate<br>Cookies<br>Pies<br>Waffles |
| **Cloves** | Beef<br>Ham<br>Pork<br>Sausage | Chicken<br>Duck<br>Fish | Beans<br>Beets<br>Onions<br>Sweet potatoes<br>Tomatoes<br>Winter squash | Apples<br>Bananas<br>Citrus fruit<br>Cranberries<br>Peaches<br>Pears | Cookies<br>Fruitcake<br>Gingerbread<br>Mincemeat<br>Steamed pudding<br>Sweet breads |
| **Ginger** | Barbecue<br>Corned beef<br>Meat loaf<br>Pot roast<br>Veal | Chicken<br>Poultry stews<br>Turkey | Beets<br>Carrots<br>Pumpkin<br>Sweet potatoes<br>Winter squash | Apples<br>Bananas<br>Figs<br>Pears<br>Pineapple | Cookies<br>Gingerbread<br>Indian pudding<br>Pies<br>Spice cake |
| **Mustard** | Beef/Veal<br>Cheese spread<br>Ham/Pork<br>Sausage | Chicken<br>Deviled eggs<br>Omelets<br>Seafood | Any vegetable,<br>  when mixed in<br>butter or sauce | Fruit salad<br>  dressings | Biscuits |

| Spice/Herb | Meat/Dairy | Fish/Eggs/Poultry | Vegetables | Fruit | Breads/Sweets |
|---|---|---|---|---|---|
| **Nutmeg** | Cheese fondue | Chicken | Carrots | Bananas | Cakes |
|  | Ground meat | Oysters | Cauliflower | Cherries | Cookies |
|  | Sausage |  | Chinese peas | Peaches | Custard pie |
|  |  |  | Green beans | Pears | Doughnuts |
|  |  |  | Spinach | Prunes | Muffins |
|  |  |  | Summer squash | Rhubarb | Puddings |
| **Oregano** | Beef/Veal | Eggs | Bean salads |  |  |
|  | Italian dishes | Fish | Green beans |  |  |
|  | Mexican dishes | Game birds | Guacamole |  |  |
|  | Pork | Turkey | Mushrooms |  |  |
| **Paprika** | Beef/Veal | Fish | Beans | Fruit salads |  |
|  | Cheese mixture | Omelets | Cabbage | Fruit salad |  |
|  | Pork | Poultry | Cauliflower | dressings |  |
|  | Sour cream mixes |  | Corn |  |  |
|  |  |  | Potatoes |  |  |
| **Parsley** | Meat loaf | Chicken pies | Asparagus |  | Biscuits |
|  | Meat pies | Fish | Beets |  | Breads |
|  | Stews | Turkey | Eggplant |  | Stuffing |
|  | Casseroles | Egg dishes | Squash |  |  |
|  | Cheese dishes |  | Dried beans |  |  |
| **Rosemary** | Beef | Chicken | Broccoli | Fruit cocktail | Ham biscuits |
|  | Italian dishes | Rabbit | Brussels | Jam |  |
|  | Pork | Salmon | Sprouts | Jelly |  |
|  | Veal |  | Cabbage |  |  |
|  |  |  | Potatoes |  |  |
| **Sage** | Roast meat | Chicken | Beans |  | Stuffing |
|  | Meat loaf | Turkey | Beets |  |  |
|  | Stews | Duck | Onions |  |  |
|  | Casseroles |  | Peas |  |  |
|  | Egg dishes |  | Spinach |  |  |
|  | Cheese dishes |  | Squash |  |  |
|  | Gravies/Sauces |  | Tomatoes |  |  |
| **Thyme** | All meats | Duck | Beans |  |  |
|  | Cheese mixture | Poultry | Spinach |  |  |
|  | Wild Game | Scrambled eggs | Tomatoes |  |  |
|  | Liver | Shellfish | Zucchini |  |  |

 **Answer the following question.**

2.9    Vegetables are classified according to how they _____ .

**Match each vegetable according to how it grows.**

| | | |
|---|---|---|
| 2.10 | _____ cabbage | a. root |
| 2.11 | _____ rhubarb | b. stem |
| 2.12 | _____ squash | c. flower |
| 2.13 | _____ beets | d. seed |
| 2.14 | _____ broccoli | e. leafy |
| 2.15 | _____ carrots | |
| 2.16 | _____ beans | |
| 2.17 | _____ cauliflower | |
| 2.18 | _____ spinach | |
| 2.19 | _____ celery | |
| 2.20 | _____ potatoes | |
| 2.21 | _____ corn | |
| 2.22 | _____ lettuce | |

**Answer the following questions.**

2.23 Which is best—plain, fresh or frozen vegetables? _____

2.24 The rule of thumb is that vegetables grown underground should be cooked _____,
and vegetables grown above ground should be cooked _____ .

2.25 If you double the vegetable recipe, increase the liquids, herbs, and spices by _____ .

2.26 Why should you wait to add the salt just before you serve the vegetables?

_____

**Complete the following activity.**

2.27 Prepare fresh broccoli steamed and then boiled. Which tasted the best?_____

Which one is crunchier? _____ Which one best retained its color?_____

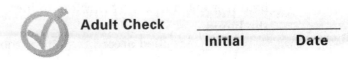

Adult Check _____

Initial          Date

25

**Fruits.** Fruits, like vegetables, are classified according to how they grow. Study the following chart.

| TYPES OF FRUITS | | |
|---|---|---|
| **Trees** | apples<br>apricots<br>avocados<br>cherries<br>dates<br>figs<br>grapefruit<br>lemons<br>limes | mangos<br>nectarines<br>oranges<br>peaches<br>pears<br>persimmons<br>plums<br>tangerines |
| **Tall bushes** | bananas<br>papaya | |
| **Bushes** | blueberries<br>cranberries<br>raspberries | |
| **Vines** | grapes<br>melons (cantaloupe, honeydew, watermelon)<br>some types of berries | |
| **Plants close to the ground** | pineapple<br>strawberries | |

Fruits can be eaten fresh, which is by far the tastiest way. We look forward to each season's fruits with anticipation. The summer's juicy peaches, sweet berries, cooling melons, and the winter's crisp apples all satisfy a hunger. When fresh fruit is not available, then canned, frozen and dried fruits are easily found.

Fruits add flavor and color to mousse, soufflés, tarts, cobblers, and preserves. Fresh fruit can be served as an appetizer, in a salad, or as a dessert.

Helpful hints for preparing and serving fruit:

1.  Don't wash fruit for storing; put it in the refrigerator dry and it will keep longer. Wash it prior to eating or using.

2.  If you are going to add fruit to cake or pudding batters, it will be less likely to sink to the bottom if you heat it in the oven first.

3.  The syrup in which canned fruits are packed is often labeled light, heavy, or extra-heavy. This refers to increasing amounts of sugar in the liquid.

4. Fruits that are cut up for salad will keep their natural color if you sprinkle them well with lemon juice.

5. Any fruit you can eat, you can drink. All you need is a blender. Depending on the fruit, you can add water, milk, honey, lemon or lime juice, or anything else that appeals to you. Invent your own fruit punch. A little yogurt is really tasty as well.

6. Fresh pineapple contains an enzyme which prevents gelatin from setting. If you want to use pineapple in a gelatin dish, either used canned or, for fresh pineapple, parboil it first for five minutes.

**Fill in the blanks.**

2.28   Apples, apricots, oranges, and figs are all examples of fruit that grows on _____.

2.29   Bananas and papaya grow on _____.

2.30   Blueberries, cranberries, and raspberries grow on _____.

2.31   Grapes and melons grow on _____.

2.32   Pineapples and strawberries grow on _____.

2.33   Fruit packed in which kind of syrup would contain the most sugar? _____.

**Complete the following activity.**

2.34   Prepare a **FRESH** fruit salad or an ambrosia salad. Write the recipe below.

**Adult Check** _____

**Initial          Date**

•Note: Make sure fruit is fresh.

27

**Dairy.** Milk is the basis for such foods as ice cream, yogurt, and cheeses. It is the main ingredient in creamed soups, gravies and sauces, puddings and custards. Milk is used in many recipes.

Cooking hints about milk.

1.  It must be cooked at a very low heat. You should not boil milk; it should only be "scalded." Scalded milk is milk that has been heated until bubbles form a ring around the top. Heat no more than this, or you will have boiled milk.

2.  When you add milk to flour mixtures, mixed vegetables or anything containing starch, warm the milk first and it will have less tendency to form lumps.

3.  When you make a cream of tomato soup which contains milk or cream, you can prevent curdling if you add the tomato to the milk, rather than vice versa.

4.  It is not necessary to throw milk away once it sours. Don't drink it, but it's safe to use in cooking. Use it right away in cake batter or cookie dough (add 1/2 teaspoon of baking soda to your flour), or in pancake batter. Or, use it in recipes calling for buttermilk in a cooked dish.

Various milk drinks are especially valuable because they are a means of getting more milk into the diets of both children and adults. In hot cocoa and chocolate, chilled cocoa or chocolate milk, milk shakes, malted milks, and eggnog, milk plays the most important role. Recently fruit "smoothies" have become favorites of people of all ages. Combining milk, fruit, ice cream or frozen yogurt, with or without crushed ice is a delicious way to get nutrients into your diet.

Yogurt is a milk product low in fat, therefore, low in calories. Many of the flavored yogurts you buy in stores contain imitation flavoring and coloring. Why not buy plain yogurt and do the flavoring yourself? Add any fruits or berries you like, as well as honey, jam, syrups, etc.

Yogurt contains less fat than sour cream. Substitute it for sour cream in baking as well as in custards, salad dressings, and sauces. Mix plain yogurt with mayonnaise, other salad dressings or your own oil and vinegar mixture for a zippy salad dressing. Try using a cup of yogurt in place of a cup of water in a gelatin dessert.

Cheese is one of the most valuable of our foods. Besides being full of flavor which blends well with a great variety of other foods, it is very high in food value; four ounces of American cheese contains almost the same amount of high-quality protein and calcium as a full quart of whole milk. The reason for this high food value is that cheese contains the solid parts of milk, including all its protein and minerals. It is a better source of Vitamin A than milk.

The character of cheese, in both texture and flavor, depends to a considerable degree on its age as well as on its variety. Very young cheeses, such as cottage cheese and cream cheese, are bland in flavor and very soft. These two types are both sour milk cheeses, which are not cured but are eaten as soon as they are produced. Most cured cheeses are aged for a few weeks to several years, before they reach their full flavor. In general, the longer they are aged the sharper their flavor is and the drier their texture.

# TYPES OF CHEESES

| | |
|---|---|
| **Hard Cheeses** do not develop their great flavors until they have been aged for at least one year. As they age, the moisture evaporates and the taste intensifies. They will keep for months if well wrapped and stored in the lower part of the refrigerator. | Jack cheese (dry)<br>Parmigiana-Reggiano<br>Romano |
| **Semi-firm Cheeses** fall into several categories, including the Swiss and French cheeses with their nutty taste and mild fragrance. They are made from either sheep or cow's milk and are pressed to achieve a firm yet supple texture. The Cheddars vary greatly in color and sharpness. | Appenzeller<br>Cheddar<br>Emmentaler |
| **Blue Cheeses** have flavor-producing molds injected during the cheese's curing process to create the veins. The cheeses age in caves where the dampness transforms the curds into a beautiful ivory color. They range from soft, creamy and mild to intense and firm. Although most blue cheeses are made from cow's milk, Roquefort is made from sheep's milk. | Bleu d'Auvergne<br>Bleu de Bresse<br>Bresse Blue<br>Roquefort |
| **Semi-soft Cheeses** are buttery and smooth in flavor and tender to the touch | Gouda and Edam<br>Provolone |
| **Soft-ripening Cheese** contain 50% butterfat and start off with a semi-soft consistency. They are fully ripe and ready to serve when they have a creamy consistency throughout. | Brie<br>Camembert |
| **Double and Triple-Cream Cheese** are smooth and creamy and tend to be very delicate. The double creams contain-60% butterfat and the triple creams between 70 and 75%. | Belletoile<br>Corolle<br>L'Explorateur<br>Saga Blue |
| **Chevres** are goat cheeses that are fresh, tangy, and zesty. They come in a multitude of shapes, ranging from pyramids and cones to logs and disks. They are dipped in brandy, wrapped in chestnut or grape leaves, and some are laced with spices and herbs. | Aged goat Cheese<br>Banon<br>Blue Westfield Farm Capri<br>Crottin |
| **Sheep's Milk Cheeses** are usually grouped with chevre for they both have a fuller flavor and saltier taste than cow's-milk cheese. One of the most famous sheep's milk-cheeses, Roquefort-is grouped with blues. Others come packed in brine or aged to a hard grating cheese. | Feta<br>Kasseri |

The protein of cheese is toughened by high temperatures and over-cooking. Cheese dishes should be  d either at a low temperature or for a very short time at a high temperature.

 eese that is cooked at too high a temperature in such a dish as macaroni and cheese, which requires a fairly long baking period, will become stringy and difficult to digest. If the oven temperature is cut down and the cooking time increased, the results will be not only more wholesome but more **palatable** too.

On the other hand, cheese that is grated and used for topping au gratin dishes may be browned, when required at quite a high temperature without ill effects if it is subjected to this high temperature for only a few minutes.

In other words, if the temperature is high, let the cooking time be short; if the cooking time must be prolonged, have the temperature low.

● ● ● ● ● ● ● ● ● ● ● ● ● ● ● ● ● ● ● ● ● ● ● ● ● ● ● ● ● ● ● ● ● ● ● ● ● ● ● ● ● ● ● ● ● ● ● ● ● ● ● ● ● ● ● ● ● ● ● ● ● ● ● ● ◀

**Answer the following questions.**

2.35    Define "scalded" milk. _____

2.36    When you make cream of tomato soup do you add the tomato to the milk or the milk to the tomato? _____

2.37    What is yogurt? _____

2.38    Yogurt is a good substitute for _____ in baking custards or making salad dressings.

2.39    Cheese contains all the solid parts of milk, including all its _____ and _____ .

2.40    The character of cheese depends on its _____ as well as its variety.

2.41    What do blue cheeses have injected into them that gives them their distinct flavor?
_____ .

2.42    When cooking cheese, if the temperature is _____ , let the cooking time be short, if the cooking time must be prolonged, have the temperature _____ .

**Answer** *true* **or** *false*.

2.43    _____ If milk begins to go a bit sour you should throw it out.

**Complete the following activity.**

2.44    Prepare your favorite recipe of baked macaroni and cheese. DO NOT use a prepared box dinner. Copy the recipe you used in the space below.

_____

_____

_____

_____

•Note: The student is to make a recipe of macaroni and cheese from scratch. Make sure the cheese has not been overcook or appears stringy. Is the cheese melted and evenly distributed throughout the dish? Check the doneness of the pasta; i rubbery, crunchy or tender. It should be tender.

Adult Check    _____
                Initial        Date

30

**Protein.** Study the meat charts in your cookbooks and learn from which part of the animal a particular cut comes. You should learn to recognize a cut on sight. The less exercise a muscle gets, the more flavorful it becomes. The most naturally flavorful cuts are from the loin area (tenderloin, strip loin or t-bone). The illustration below is a chart butchers use which shows the various cuts of meat and where they may be found on the animal.

There are many factors that affect a beef-buying decision. The first is the grade or brand stamp. The grade refers to the eating quality. The USDA has a voluntary meat grading service for which they charge a fee to the firm (usually a meat packer) requesting the service. You should become familiar with the top three of the eight beef grades—USDA PRIME, CHOICE, and SELECT—because these are the grades most likely to be seen at the meat counter. All three grades are from young, well-fed animals, less than two years old. The other beef grades are sold as ungraded or used in processed meats, sausages, and canned meats.

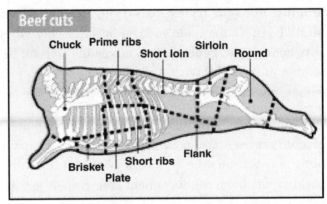

PRIME:    This beef is the highest quality; most tender, juicy, and flavorful.

CHOICE:   This beef is the most popular quality, very tender, juicy, and flavorful. Choice grade is produced in the greatest volume.

SELECT:   This beef is lean and fairly tender. Because it has less marbling, it lacks some of the juiciness and flavor of the higher grades.

The second thing you need to check when buying meat is its appearance. Marbling is the fine white streaks of fat running throughout the lean meat. The PRIME grade has the best overall eating quality because it has the most marbling. Marbling contributes to tenderness, taste, and juiciness.

Trim is the moderated fat covering most of the exterior of beef cuts and helps in retaining juices while the beef is cooking. In roasts, the fat covering acts as a self baster. The trim should be firm and white and no more than 1/8 inch thick on steaks and 1/4 inch on roasts.

Connective tissue or gristle differs from marbling; it is not evenly distributed throughout the meat and the heavier strands are like translucent ribbons. It does not dissolve easily when cooked and is hard to chew. Moist heat is required to tenderize or soften this gristle.

Another part of the appearance to check is the color of the meat. When beef is first cut, it is dark reddish purple in color, but within minutes its surface quickly turns to a bright red in the presence of oxygen. The color of the lean beef should be light red to red, unless it is cured, aged or smoked.

When buying beef you should ask about aging. Beef improves with aging. The term *aging* simply means the length of time beef cuts are stored under controlled temperature and humidity before they are packaged for the meat counter. Dry aging is practiced under carefully controlled conditions. Wet aging is more common and occurs in vacuum bags under refrigerated temperatures. Beef aging significantly increases tenderness. It varies from 3–21 days or 10–14 for the best quality. Note, beef cannot be aged in your refrigerator at home.

The tenderness of a beef cut determines the method or methods of cooking to insure eating satisfaction. Tender cuts are best when cooked by DRY HEAT methods such as roasting, broiling, barbecuing, pan-broiling, deep-fat frying, pan-frying, and stir-frying. Less tender cuts are made tender by cooking with MOIST HEAT methods such as braising (pot-roasts and stews), cooking in liquid, slow cooking, and pressure cooking. In general, it is advisable to cook beef slowly at a low temperature which results in a more tender, juicy, and flavorful product. On the following page is a chart that will determine the location of the cuts, types of meat found in each section of the beef and the best method for cooking each cut.

Roasting is a dry heat method of cooking and is reserved for the most tender of cuts. Place a large cut of meat (at least two pounds) on a rack with the fat side up. The melting fat will baste the meat as it cooks, but the roast must be on a rack so that it doesn't stew in its own fat. Bone-in roasts take less time to cook because the bone conducts heat. You can either start a roast at a high temperature to sear the outside and seal in the juices or roast at a constant moderate (300° to 350°) temperature. Save the pan juices for gravy. All roasts should stand at least 15 minutes before carving to allow the juices to settle.

Broiling is another dry heat method for tender cuts. Steaks and chops can be broiled, but never whole roasts. Place the oven rack three to four inches from the heat. Some less tender steaks can be broiled if they are marinated (which starts breaking down tough muscle fibers), cooked just to rare or medium-rare and then thinly sliced across the grain. London broil is great prepared this way.

Pan-broiling also uses fast dry heat, but the heat comes from the pan. Heat a dry heavy skillet over medium to medium-high heat until very hot. Pat the meat dry and add it to the skillet and brown on both sides, checking the center for doneness and adjusting the heat to maintain a lively sizzle. Pour off the drippings as they collect and turn the meat frequently.

Pan-frying or sautéing is just like pan-broiling except that a little fat is added to the pan first.

Braising is a moist-heat method of cooking for tough (or less tender) cuts of meat. A little liquid is added to the pan, the pan is tightly covered and the meat is cooked in a slow oven or over low heat on top of the stove.

**One way to serve beef.**

## BEEF CUTS AND METHODS OF COOKING

| Beef Cut | Meat Type | Method of Cooking |
|---|---|---|
| **Chuck/shoulder** | Arm pot-roast or steak | Braise |
| | 7-Bone pot-roast or steak | Braise |
| | Blade roast or steak | Braise, broil or pan-broil |
| | Cross rib pot roast boneless | Braise |
| | Shoulder pot roast boneless | Braise |
| | Short ribs | Braise, cook in liquid |
| **Brisket, Shank, and Plate** | Beef brisket | Braise, cook in liquid |
| | Beef shank soup bones | Cook in liquid |
| | Beef shank cross cuts | Braise, cook in liquid |
| | Beef plate steak rolls boneless | Braise, broil, pan-broil, pan-fry |
| | Beef plate short ribs | Braise, cook in liquid |
| **Rib** | Rib roast | Roast |
| | Rib steak | Broil, pan-broil, pan-fry |
| | Rib eye roast | Roast |
| | Rib eye steak | Broil, pan-broil, pan-fry |
| | Short ribs | Braise, cook in liquid |
| **Flank** | Beef flank steak | Broil, braise |
| | Beef flank steak rolls | Braise, broil, pan-broil, pan-fry |
| **Round, Rump** | Tip steak or roast | Broil, pan-broil, pan-fry, braise, Roast if high quality |
| | Round steak | Braise, pan-fry |
| | Top round steak or roast | Broil, pan-broil, pan-fry |
| | Bottom round steak or roast | Braise, pan-fry, braise or roast if high quality |
| | Eye round steak or roast | Braise, pan-broil, pan-fry, Braise or roast if high quality |
| | Rump roast | Braise, roast if high quality |
| | Heel of round | Braise, cook in liquid |
| | Cubes for kabobs | Braise, broil |
| **Loin** | T-bone steak | Broil, pan-broil, pan-fry |
| | Porterhouse steak | Broil, pan-broil, pan-fry |
| | Tenderloin steak | Broil, pan-broil, pan-fry |
| | Sirloin steaks | Broil, pan-broil, pan-fry |
| | Tenderloin roast | Roast |

**Complete the following crossword puzzle.**

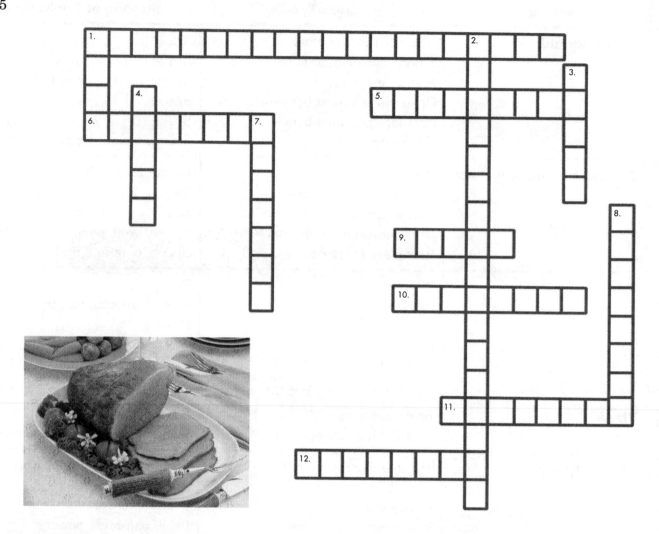

**Across:**

1. range of time for beef aging (5 words)
5. uses a little hot fat
6. fine white streaks of fat
9. quality measurement
10. dry heat cooking, reserved for most tender cuts
11. dry heat where you cook directly under or over the source of heat
12. dry heat method of cooking where the heat comes from a pan.

**Down:**

1. fat covering most of the exterior of the beef
2. the original color of beef when first cut (3 words)
3. length of time beef is stored in controlled temperature and humidity.
4. highest quality beef according to USDA grading
7. tough connective tissue
8. moist heat method of cooking for tough cuts of meats

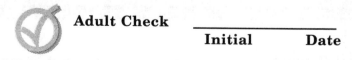

**Adult Check** _____

**Initial**          **Date**

# FAMILY AND CONSUMER SCIENCE

**three**

## LIFEPAC TEST

78 / 98

**Name** _____

**Date** _____

**Score** _____

# FAMILY AND CONSUMER SCIENCE 03: LIFEPAC TEST

**Choose the correct answer** (each answer, 2 points).

1.      The average person needs _____ servings from the milk group daily.
        a.  2–3                              b.  4–6
        c.  6–8

2.      The best sources of protein are _____ .
        a.  whole-meal grain products        b.  leafy vegetables and citrus
        c.  meats, eggs, cheese, and fish

3.      The best sources of Vitamin C are _____ .
        a.  citrus fruits and leafy vegetables    b.  macaroni, rice, and grain-based food
        c.  fish, shellfish, other seafood

4.      Among the best sources of calcium are _____ .
        a.  beef, chicken, or turkey products     b.  whole-meal grain products
        c.  milk/dairy products

5.      The human body derives energy from which of the following _____ .
        a.  carbohydrates                    b.  proteins
        c.  fats                             d.  all of the above

6.      The "sunshine" vitamin is _____ .
        a.  Vitamin A                        b.  Vitamin C
        c.  Vitamin D

7.      One of the best sources of iron is _____ .
        a.  milk                             b.  dry beans
        c.  liver

8.      The average person should have _____ glasses of water each day.
        a.  2–4                              b.  6–8
        c.  10–12

9.      Best sources of Vitamin A are _____ .
        a.  green and yellow vegetables      b.  fruits
        c.  milk

**Match the letter of the nutrient with its function** (each answer, 1 point).

10.     _____ helps resist infection                    a.  calcium

11.     _____ for good eyesight                         b.  Vitamin C

12.     _____ formation of bones and teeth              c.  iodine

13.     _____ for building strong bones and teeth       d.  iron

14.     _____ for healthy red blood cells               e.  Vitamin A

15.     _____ control of thyroid gland                  f.  Vitamin B

16.     _____ helps promote proper digestion            g.  Vitamin D

**Answer** *true* **or** *false* (each answer, 1 point).

17. _____ When you serve a blue plate meal, the guests are seated and the food is passed around the table.

18. _____ When designing a meal, you should choose the main dish first.

19. _____ Vegetables are high in vitamins and minerals.

20. _____ Beaten egg yolks are a good leavening agent used in cakes.

21. _____ Frostings are thicker than icings.

22. _____ Bread left to rise too long will be mushroom-shaped.

23. _____ If you use too little shortening, the pastry becomes tough.

24. _____ The texture of a good baked pastry should be blistery, pebbly, and flaky.

25. _____ Flour and liquid when mixed together produce gluten.

26. _____ Yeast, through fermentation, produces oxygen gas that leavens the dough.

27. _____ The Dietary Guide for Americans recommends that people choose a diet that includes oils but is low in fat, saturated fat, and cholesterol.

28. _____ Foods that are fats, oils, and sweets add mostly calories to the diet.

29. _____ Vitamins that cannot be stored by the body are water soluble.

30. _____ Fresh is always best when serving vegetables plain.

31. _____ Beef improves with aging.

32. _____ The important rule to remember when placing knives is that the cutting edge should be placed toward the plate.

33. _____ The dessert fork and spoon belong at the top of the plate.

34. _____ Foods are passed to the left, clockwise.

35. _____ Clean off breads, salt, pepper, and condiments after the last course but before dessert.

**Fill in the blank(s)** (each answer, 3 points).

36. Vegetables and fruits are classified by how they are _____ .

37. _____ is the leavening agent for an angel food cake.

38. The function of _____ in a pastry is to add tenderness, richness, and flakiness.

39. Rice should be rinsed before cooking to remove _____ with which it is coated.

40. The most tender cuts of meat are cooked using the dry method of _____ .

41. Cooking is an art that appeals to all _____ .

42. The _____ style of service has seven courses.

43. Complete proteins are found in foods that come from _____ sources.

2

44. Vitamins are substances that are needed by the body for _____ and
_____ .

45. Two things that affect nutrient needs are _____ and _____ .

46. If you double the vegetable recipe, increase the liquid, herbs, and spices by less than
_____ .

47. The beef which is highest in quality, most tender and juicy, and most flavorful is labeled with
_____ grade.

48. _____ is the fine white streaks of fat running throughout the lean meat.

49. A _____ salad is sweet rather than tart and served after the meal is finished.


**Define the following words** (each answer, 2 points).

50. trace minerals _____

51. marinating _____

52. cover _____

When roasting a whole chicken or turkey, use the roasting bags available at the grocery store. They are not only very easy to use, but they trap the nutrients and flavor right in the bag. The meat is usually tender and juicy if you follow the instructions that come with the bags. Save the juice to make gravy.

When you sauté or pan-fry chicken, heat the fat only moderately hot. Chicken sautéd in fat that is too hot gets an unpleasant flavor. Cook it skin-side down at the start so that the skin won't shrivel before it has cooked and browned. Dark meat takes a little longer to cook than light. When you sauté chicken, cook the thighs and legs about four minutes longer than other parts of the bird. To check for doneness, prick with a sharp-tined fork; if the juice which rises is clear and untinged with pink, it's cooked enough.

When you bread or flour chicken pieces before frying, refrigerate them for one hour or more and you'll find that the covering will adhere better during cooking.

If you fry chicken pieces in deep fat, watch for them to rise to the surface. This indicates that they are done. You'll see that they are a nice golden brown.

The dark meat of a chicken is more flavorful than the light meat. So if you are making soup or stew, the dark meat will give it a richer taste.

The healthiest ways to prepare chicken are broiled, grilled or baked; preparing chicken in fat such as sauteing, deep frying or pan frying is less so. Think healthy.

Americans are hooked on seafood. We are eating more of it than ever before and for a good reason; fresh-flavored, quick to prepare and healthy for us, fish and shellfish fit perfectly with today's lifestyle.

Fish has delicate flesh and dries out easily. Never overcook. The moment it flakes easily with a fork, it's done. If the fish is thick, separate the flesh deep inside and examine it. When it loses its **translucency**, it's done. Fish can be broiled, sauteed, baked, grilled or poached.

---

**Answer the following questions.**

2.46    What are two factors to consider when buying beef? _____

2.47    What things do you need to consider with the appearance of beef? _____

_____

2.48    What determines the method of cooking beef? _____

2.49    Tender cuts should be cooked by _____ methods and less tender cuts should be cooked by _____ methods.

2.50    Why does it take less time for a roast with the bone left in than a boneless roast to cook?

_____

2.51　Why should a chicken be pan fried in moderately hot fat rather than hot fat?

_____

2.52　How can you tell when the pan-fried chicken is done? _____

2.53　How can you tell when fish is done? _____

---

Marinating makes meat even tastier. Prepare a marinating sauce for meat, fish or chicken the day before you need it. This allows the flavors to blend and enhance one another. Place the meat and the **marinade** in a large zippered plastic bag, put in a large bowl and turn it now and then. It will take 2–24 hours depending on the size of the meat. If the piece of meat to be marinated is very large, prick it with a sharp fork here and there to allow the marinade to penetrate the meat. Marinades traditionally contain some sort of acid ingredient such as vinegar, wine, citrus juice or tomato. Most marinades contain oil which helps the cooking of beef cuts with little natural fat.

You can use almost any salad dressing made with flavored oil and vinegar, lemon or lime as a marinade for ripe olives, fresh or canned mushrooms, and many vegetables (if you blanch them first), including cauliflowerets, green or yellow beans, green or red sweet peppers, and onions. Let them marinate in the dressing for a day or so.

**Answer the following questions.**

2.54　What is a marinade? _____

2.55　Why use a marinade on your meats?_____

**Complete the following activity.**

2.56　Prepare your favorite recipe of beef and vegetable stew. Do not use a canned stew. Start with fresh foods. Copy the recipe used in the space below.

```
_____
_____
_____
_____
_____
_____
```

•Note: Make sure the meat is tender and juicy, the vegetables are done but not mushy and the flavor is pleasing.

 **Adult Check** _____

Initial　　　　Date

Now that we have covered preparing foods from MyPlate, look at some specialty items: soups, salads, and garnishes.

No food is quite like soup. It fills your whole home with its great aroma and lovingly draws friends and family into the kitchen. Nourishing and comforting, soup is loved by both young and old. A most versatile food, soup is the perfect way to balance a menu. The nutritional value of soup is based on what is in the soup. Serve a light, appetite-stimulating consommé or bouillon to elegantly complement a rich main course, or if the main course is light, serve a more substantial pureed vegetable soup to round out the meal. Creamed soups, cheese soups or hearty vegetable, and beef soups are filling and can be served on their own as main dishes.

There are two types of soup: a stock soup, which is a clear soup using bone and meat as a base; and mild-based soup, which is a cream soup and uses milk as a base. Listed below are four basic kinds of soup.

- *Bouillon* is a clear soup or broth made from beef or chicken.

- *Bisque* is a rich cream soup made from pureed seafood, fish or vegetables.

- *Chowder* is a mild based soup or stew using fish, seafood, or vegetables. Two favorites are corn chowder and clam chowder.

- *Consommé* is a clear soup made from boiling meat, bones, and sometimes vegetables.

With the availability of many wonderful varieties of lettuce, salad has become a great way to eat a delicious dish with healthy ingredients. During the summer, when the heat waves cause a dip in our appetites, salads have become the focal point of our meals.

Salads are usually grouped according to their place in the daily menu. Listed below are four types of salads, their descriptions, and examples of each.

- An *appetizer* is a small to medium sized crisp salad with tangy dressing; served at the beginning of a meal to stimulate the appetite. Examples are fresh, tart fruit; seafood with a tangy sauce served on lettuce.

- An *accompaniment* is a small to medium sized salad that contrasts in flavor, color and texture with the rest of the meal. It is served with the main course. Examples are tossed salad, coleslaw, and bean salad.

- A *main dish* is a hearty and satisfying salad built around protein food; served as the main course. Examples are chicken salad, chef's salad, and tuna salad.

- A *dessert or party salad* is a sweet rather than a tart salad served after the meal is finished. Examples are molded fruit or mixed fruit topped with coconut and whipped cream.

There are simply four parts to a salad. The base is the lower layer of the ingredients which adds contrast in color and texture and keeps the salad from looking bare. The base of the salad is placed on the plate first and is usually some kind of greens, such as lettuce. The *body* is the major part of the salad and gives the salad its name; for example, gelatin salad. The *salad dressing* makes up the combined ingredients that are added to the salad to enhance flavor, color and taste appeal or to bind the ingredients together. The last part of a salad is the *garnish,* which is food used to decorate another food. Examples of garnishes are carrot curls, radish roses, parsley, tomato peel roses, lemon wedges, pickle fans, and celery curls.

There are three basic salad dressings. *The French-type dressing* is an oil-based dressing that will pour from the bottle. Examples of French-type dressings are French, creamy Italian, Caesar, and vinegar and oil. *Mayonnaise-type dressings* are thick, oil-based dressings that must be spooned rather than poured. Examples are thousand island and bleu cheese. The *cooked-egg* dressings are cornstarch or flour-based dressings and are used mostly by gourmet cooks.

Listed below are factors to consider when preparing salads.

**A colorful fruit salad.**

1. Select highest quality of vegetables and fruits whose flavors blend together. Vegetables should be firm, colorful and free from blemish and decay. Fruits should be firm, juicy, flavorful and free from blemish.

2. Wash raw vegetables thoroughly before combining into a salad. Some vegetables such as carrots will require scraping after washing.

3. Chop, dice, shred, tear, or slice salad ingredients to make bite-size pieces. (Review these words from LIFEPAC 2.)

4. Cook vegetables just until done. Overcooking will cause loss of nutrient, color, and desired texture. Examples are potato salad and three bean salad.

5. Prepare salad (except gelatin or salads requiring special preparation) just before serving. Vitamin C is rapidly lost from raw vegetables and fruits which are cut and left standing at room temperature. If it is necessary to prepare salad ahead of time, cover well, and refrigerate.

6. Select a salad dressing to compliment and blend with the salad and meal.

7. Serve salads at appropriate temperatures. Hot salads should be served hot; cold salads should be served cold on cold plates. Salads containing meat, mayonnaise or eggs should be kept refrigerated or chilled before, during, and after serving to prevent food spoilage.

8. Drain salad ingredients thoroughly before combining ingredients.

9. Dissolve gelatin used in salads according to package directions. When planning to add fruits and/or other ingredients to gelatin, do not add all of the liquid that is recommended. Follow recipe instructions to determine the amount of water to be added.

Garnishes are used in cooking to decorate food, making it more attractive. They add contrast in color, shape, and texture. They also add flavor. Garnishes are great because they are edible, inexpensive, and add glamour to an otherwise economical meal. Be an artist when you garnish. Follow the principles of good design: aim for balance, choose compatible colors, and have a pleasing arrangement. Properly clean the food and don't over-garnish. Use a variety of garnishes, both plain and fancy. Be creative—experiment but most definitely get in the habit of garnishing your food. The extra minutes are worth it.

**Answer the following questions.**

2.57 What are the two types of soup? _____

2.58 List and describe the four basic kinds of soup.

a. _____

b. _____

c. _____

d. _____

2.59 Which kind of salad is served with the main course? _____

2.60 Mixed fruit topped with coconut and whipped cream is an example of which kind of salad?

_____

2.61 What does salad dressing do for a salad? _____

2.62 What are the three basic salad dressings? a. _____ , b. _____ ,
and  c. _____

2.63 Define garnishes. Give two examples. _____
a. _____ , b. _____

**Complete the following activity.**

2.64 Prepare a salad or soup of your choice. Show skill in using garnish. Copy the recipe used in the space below.

•Note: Be sure to check to see that the student has used some kind of garnish

**Adit Check** _____
**Adult Check**
**Initial**      **Date**

# BAKING

Everyone loves the aroma that comes from the kitchen when something good is baking in the oven. This section of the LIFEPAC is devoted to baking those scrumptious foods: cookies, cakes, pastry, pies, and breads.

**Cookies.** Have you ever been caught with your hand in the cookie jar? Snacking on cookies is an ageless activity. Without a doubt, cookies are America's favorite sweet snack and we have adapted recipes from all over the world, from peanut butter to chocolate chip to raisin oatmeal.

The perfect cookie should have good flavor and tender crumbs, unless the variety is a hard cookie. Texture may be soft or crisp, depending upon the variety of cookie, with a uniform color and shape. Cookies are classified in three ways—by the texture of the baked cookie (soft or crisp), the consistency of the batter or dough (soft or stiff), or by the method used in shaping the cookie. We are going to look at six types of cookies.

*Drop* cookies have a soft, drop batter consistency. They are dropped from a spoon onto a baking sheet about 2 inches apart. Some are flattened and some are not. Examples are date, drop, and chocolate chip.

*Refrigerator* cookie dough is rich in shortening and sugar. It is shaped into rolls or blocks and chilled in the refrigerator for several hours. Thin slices are cut and baked. Examples are peanut butter, molasses, pinwheels or a basic refrigerator cookie recipe.

*Bar* cookies are baked as a sheet in a shallow pan, cooled, and cut into squares or bars. Examples are chocolate chip bars, brownies or gumdrop cookies.

*Molded* cookie dough is formed into small balls and flattened with a fork or other utensil to form designs. Examples are oatmeal, peanut butter, and coconut cookies.

*Rolled* cookies require stiff dough that is rolled out on a lightly floured board to a desired thickness and cut into shapes. Examples are sugar and butter cookies. These are fun to make and decorate for special holidays such as Christmas and Valentine's Day. You can also use this recipe to make filled cookies and pinwheels.

*Pressed* cookies are made from a soft dough that is put into a cookie press and squeezed out to form fancy shapes. You can use a butter cookie recipe and add flavors or colors to it.

The steps in making cookies:

1.  Preheat the oven.

2.  Arrange all needed equipment conveniently.

3.  Assemble all ingredients.

4.  Melt chocolate over hot water, if recipe calls for chocolate.

5.  Prepare the cookie sheets according to the recipe.

6.  Blend flour thoroughly with the other dry ingredients, such as salt, baking powder, baking soda, and spices.

7.  Prepare any fruits or nuts the recipe calls for.

8.  Measure shortening and liquid ingredients.

9.  Cream shortening by beating until it becomes creamy. Add sugar gradually and beat well with each addition. The mixture should have a fluffy appearance when thoroughly creamed.

10.  Add dry ingredients and beat till they are mixed in well. Continue following recipe directions.

Once the dough is ready, place the cookies evenly on the baking sheet and not too close to the edge. Remove the cookies from the oven as soon as they are slightly brown on the edges. Cookies that are overbaked will be dry and hard. Transfer them to a cooling rack at once with a spatula or pancake turner. When they are thoroughly cool, store them in containers with tightly fitted covers. Store crispy and soft cookies in separate containers.

**Answer the following questions.**

2.65    List the three ways which cookies are classified.

    a. _____

    b. _____

    c. _____

2.66    Describe the six types of cookies listed below.

    a.  drop cookies    _____

    b.  refrigerator cookies    _____

    c.  bar cookies    _____

    d.  molded cookies    _____

    e.  rolled cookies    _____

    f.  pressed cookies    _____


**Complete the following activity.**

2.67    Make a batch of cookies, using your own recipe, but following the basic steps listed above. Copy the recipe in the space below.

•Note: Check for texture, appearance, and flavor of the cookie. Does it correspond with the recipe?

 **Adult Check** _____

                                                   **Initial**      **Date**

41

**Cakes.** Cakes have been a part of the American family for generations. Everyone remembers the excitement of their birthday cake resplendent in candlelight. Cakes are a delight for any family dessert as well as all special occasions.

All cakes have the same basic ingredients: flour, sugar, shortening, eggs, leavening (baking powder, baking soda, beaten egg whites), and flavoring. They are either made with shortening (butter cakes) or without shortening (sponge or angel food cakes).

Exact measurement of all ingredients is fundamental to success, because cake texture depends largely on the balance between the various ingredients.

---

### A Thought to Ponder

Romans 8:28 says, "And we know that all things work together for good to them that love God, to them who are the called according to his purpose."

Although some ingredients that make up a cake may taste bad by themselves, a cake won't turn out if one of those ingredients is left out. God knows that our lives won't be as He has planned if one event whether sweet or bitter is left out.

---

There are some pointers that will help you be more successful in your cake baking endeavors. Select a tried-and-true recipe. Have the ingredients at room temperature. Be sure to use the right kind and size of cake pan or pans. Use the correct oven temperature and be sure the oven racks are adjusted correctly and are level. Alternate placement of pans in the oven so that no pan is directly over another pan. Watch for signs of doneness; butter cakes shrink from the sides of the pan. All cakes spring back into place when touched lightly with the finger. Place the pan on a cooling rack for 5 to 10 minutes before removing cake.

For angel food and sponge cakes, take care to handle the batter gently so as to keep the air in it, since this is the leavening agent. Allow the cake to remain in the inverted pan for one hour after removing it from the oven.

Once the cake is cooled, you are ready to frost it. Frostings are used on cakes only. They are thicker than icings and may be cooked or uncooked. Butter frostings are uncooked and are made of butter, confectioner's sugar, liquids, and flavorings. Cooked frostings are mixtures of sugar and liquid, cooked like candy. Examples are panocha, or brown-sugar frosting, and chocolate-fudge frosting.

Icings are used on cakes, breads, coffee cakes, and sweet rolls. They are thinner than frostings. Fluffy icings are cooked mixtures of sugar, corn syrup, water, and unbeaten raw egg whites. Thin icings are uncooked mixtures of confectioner's sugar and liquid, of a consistency that spreads easily. A very thin icing may be poured onto a pastry.

When decorating a cake, level the cake first, fill the layers, frost the top, frost the sides, smooth the sides and smooth the top. There are cake decorating kits for those who wish to be creative. These kits contain decorating tubes, bags, and directions. Go have some fun!

**Answer the following questions.**

2.68    What is the difference between a butter cake and an angel food cake? _____

_____

2.69    How can you tell if angel food cakes and butter cakes are done baking?_____

2.70    What is the leavening agent in an angel food cake?_____

2.71    What is the difference between frosting and icing? _____

**Complete the following activity.**

2.72    Make a cake from scratch. Do <u>not</u> use a mix. Frost it with homemade frosting, not canned. Have some fun decorating if you desire. Copy the recipes for the cake and the frosting onto the recipe card.

•Note: Check for texture, form, flavor, and appearance.

**Adult Check** _____

                                        **Initial**         **Date**

**Pastry.** Pastry is a baked product made from dough rich in fat. Examples are meat, custard, fruit pies, tarts, turnovers, and cobblers. A good pastry will have a golden brown color, uniform, attractive edge, and a blistery, pebbly surface indicating that it will be flaky when cut. It should be fairly thin, so the bottom as well as the rim will become crisp. It should be tender and easy to cut with a fork, but not so tender that it crumbles. It should hold its shape when served. It should have a pleasant, bland flavor to enhance the filling.

The ingredients used for making plain pastry dough and their functions are as follows:
1. flour, which provides framework and structure;
2. fat or shortening, which provides tenderness, richness, and flakiness;
3. salt, which adds flavor; and
4. water (or milk), which binds the ingredients together.

Nutrients contained in pastry dough are fats and carbohydrates. Nutrients provided by pastry products are determined to a large extent by the filling in the pastry. Custard and fruit pastry provide some vitamins and minerals. Main dish pastry products contribute some protein, Vitamin B, and minerals.

Not only are there plain pastry pie crusts but it should be noted that there are graham-cracker crumb, chocolate-cookie crumb, toasted grated coconut, vanilla wafer, and cheese pastry pie crusts that are quite tasty and add variety to your pies.

There are a variety of pie fillings to choose from as well. For example, meat and vegetable mixtures; milk and egg custards; milk and cornstarch custards; cooked, thickened fruit juices; cream cheese custard; baked fruit such as apple, peach, cherry, pineapple and raisin; meat and fruit such as mincemeat; fruit, gelatin and stiffly beaten egg whites, such as chiffon.

Bake a pre-baked shell at 450°–475° F for 12 to 15 minutes. Bake a shell with filling at 450°–475° F for 12 minutes and then additional time according to the requirements of each particular recipe.

**Answer the following questions.**

2.73    What are the qualities of a good pastry? _____

_____

_____

2.74    Nutrients contained in pastry dough are_____

_____

_____

**Put the name of the following ingredients of pastry in the correct space by its function.**

2.75    1. _____ provides framework and structure              a.  fat

        2. _____ binds the ingredients together                 b.  flour

        3. _____ adds flavor                                    c.  salt

        4. _____ provides tenderness, richness, and flakiness   d.  water

44

**Complete the following activity.**

2.76 Bake a pie. You will be graded on the pastry as well as the filling. Copy the recipe in the space below.

• Note: The pastry crust should be golden brown in color, have blistery surface and uniform, attractive edges. It should cut easily with a table knife but hold its shape when served. It should have a flaky texture and crisp rim. The flavor should be pleasant, but bland to enhance the flavor of the filling.

The filling will vary. In a fruit pie the fruit should be tender, have more fruit than filling and not be a canned filling. A cream pie should be smooth, have a creamy texture, not runny or separated. The flavor should be pleasing to the palate; not too sweet but not too tart.

Toppings can be a fancy double crust, whipped cream or meringue.

 **Adult Check** _____

                                                      **Initial**           **Date**

**Breads (Quick Yeast Bread).** No smell is more welcoming than that of freshly baked bread. No taste is more tantalizing then fresh, hot bread with butter melted on top. There are many different kinds of bread to choose from—yeast breads, quick breads, muffins, **popovers**, **scones**, etc. Each one is unique and delicious. We are going to concentrate on yeast bread. Please do not use a bread machine for this section.

The main nutrients contained in yeast breads are protein, carbohydrates, B vitamins, and iron. Nutrients and calories provided by yeast breads are determined to a large extent by the type of yeast bread as well as the topping and other additions.

The essential ingredients of yeast-leavened dough are flour, liquid, and yeast. Flour provides the proteins that, when hydrated and mixed, produce gluten. Gluten is responsible for **extensibility** and **elasticity** in the dough. Liquid is essential to hydrate flour proteins. Yeast through fermentation provides carbon dioxide gas that leavens the bread. Other ingredients are sugar, which increases the rate of fermentation, decreases the rising time, improves the flavor, and improves browning: fat which increases the tenderness of the bread; and salt which enhances flavor, decreases fermentation, thus increasing the time required for bread dough to rise and gives a firming effect to the gluten structure. Bread made without salt is often crumbly in texture.

The basic steps in making yeast bread are mix, knead, rise, punch down, shape, rise, bake, and cool. The amount of time the bread is left to rise will affect its shape. Rising time that is too long creates a mushroom-shaped bread with a concave center and excess dough hanging over the sides. Too short rising time leaves cracks on the sides of the bread.

Desirable characteristics of yeast bread are:

1. Evenly shaped with no humps or large cracks;
2. Tender and crisp crust;
3. Mellow flavor characteristic of ingredients;
4. Golden brown or darker color;
5. Soft, tender, and moist texture with no tunnels and
6. Pleasant odor characteristic of ingredients.

The most common uses for yeast bread dough are dinner rolls, loaf bread, dessert rolls or breads (tea ring, cinnamon rolls, bread braid), breadsticks, coffee cake, and pizza crust.

**Match the name of the ingredient in the space provided with the phrase that matches its function.**

| | | |
|---|---|---|
| 2.77 | _____ hydrates flour proteins | a. flour |
| 2.78 | _____ increases the rate of fermentation | b. yeast |
| 2.79 | _____ provides proteins; when hydrated produces gluten | c. liquid |
| 2.80 | _____ enhances the flavor | d. salt |
| 2.81 | _____ ferments, producing carbon dioxide | e. fat |
| | | f. sugar |

**Fill in the blanks.**

2.82  Gluten is responsible for _____ and _____ in the dough.

2.83  If bread is left to rise too long it will create a _____ shape with a concave

_____ and dough hanging over the edge of the pan.

**Complete the following activity.**

2.84  Make a loaf of bread. Use any recipe that is not a mix. Do not use a bread machine. Follow the basic
steps as given above in bread making. Copy the recipe used in the space below.

•Note:  The bread should be
  1.  Evenly shaped with no humps of large cracks
  2.  Tender and crisp crust
  3.  Mellow flavor characteristic of ingredients
  4.  Golden brown or darker color
  5.  Soft, tender, and moist texture with no tunnels
  6.  A pleasant odor characteristic of the ingredients

**Adult Check**  _____

Initial          Date

 Review the material in this section in preparation for the Self Test. The Self Test will check
your mastery of this particular section. The items missed on this Self Test will indicate specific
areas where restudy is needed for mastery.

# SELF TEST 2

**Fill in the blanks** (each answer, 2 points).

2.01     The most common grains used in cereals are wheat, oats, _____ and _____ .

2.02     The two groups that cereals are classified into are _____ and _____ .

2.03     The rule of thumb for vegetables grown underground, is to cook _____ and vegetables grown above ground, cook _____ .

2.04     When cooking cheese, if the temperature is _____ , let the cooking time be short; if the cooking time must be prolonged have the temperature _____ .

2.05     Vitamin D is important for strong _____ and _____ .

2.06     _____ is responsible for elasticity and extensibility in bread dough.

**Choose the correct answer** (each answer, 1 point).

2.07     What is the most important characteristic of prepared cereals? _____
      a. flavor              b. crispness             c. color

2.08     Pasta and rice will swell _____ times during cooking.
      a. 2–4               b. 3–5             c. 2–3

2.09     Vegetables and fruits are classified by how they are _____ .
      a. prepared           b. stored             c. grown

2.010    If you double the vegetable recipe, increase the liquids, herbs, and spices by less than _____ .
      a. 1/4               b. 1/2             c. 2/3

2.011    The character of cheese depends on its _____ as well as it variety.
      a. color              b. age               c. texture

2.012    Vitamin _____ helps to clot blood.
      a. A                b. B                c. K

2.013    Which mineral helps in the prevention of tooth decay? _____
      a. calcium           b. fluorine           c. iron

2.014    The leavening agent for a sponge cake or angel food cake is _____ .
      a. air               b. yeast             c. egg

2.015    The following qualities refer to a good _____ ; golden brown crust, uniform attractive edge, blistery pebbly surface.
      a. cookie           b. cake             c. pastry

2.016    The function of fat in a pastry is to _____ .
      a. provide framework and structure       b. provide tenderness, richness, and flakiness
      c. bind the ingredients together

**Answer** *True* **or** *False* (each answer, 1 point).

2.017 _____ Rinse rice before cooking to remove the loose starch with which it is coated.

2.018 _____ Cooking in salted water causes vegetables to lose their vitamin content.

2.019 _____ Frozen vegetables are better than fresh vegetables when served plain.

2.020 _____ Fruit packed in heavy syrup contains the most sugar.

2.021 _____ When you make tomato soup, you should add the milk to the tomato.

2.022 _____ Teens need at least three servings of milk each day.

2.023 _____ Milk is a great source of calcium.

2.024 _____ Blue cheese contains mold.

2.025 _____ Tender cuts of beef are best when cooked by moist heat methods.

2.026 _____ The dark meat of poultry takes longer to cook than the white meat.

2.027 _____ Bouillon is a rich, creamy soup.

2.028 _____ Salad dressing enhances the flavor, color, and taste appeal of the salad.

2.029 _____ A sponge or angel food cake has no shortening in it.

2.030 _____ Frostings are thinner than icings.

2.031 _____ Yeast ferments, producing the carbon dioxide gas that leavens bread.

**Match the vegetables** (each answer, 1 point).

2.032 _____ celery          a.   root

2.033 _____ beans           b.   stem

2.034 _____ carrots         c.   flower

2.035 _____ broccoli        d.   seed

2.036 _____ spinach         e.   leafy

**Match the fruit** (each answer, 1 point).

2.037 _____ bananas         a.   trees

2.038 _____ grapes          b.   tall bushes

2.039 _____ blueberries     c.   bushes

2.040 _____ strawberries    d.   vines

2.041 _____ apples          e.   close to the ground

**Define the following words** (each answer, 3 points).

2.042   Scalded milk   _____

2.043   Yogurt   _____

2.044   Marbling   _____

2.045   Aging of beef   _____

2.046   Marinade   _____

2.047   Garnish   _____


**Matching** (each answer, 2 points).

2.048   _____   the beef quality measurement                                              a.   pan frying

2.049   _____   dry heat method of cooking when the heat comes from a pan     b.   grade

2.050   _____   uses a little hot fat                                                       c.   roasting

2.051   _____   dry heat where you cook directly under or over the source of heat   d.   broiling

2.052   _____   moist heat method of cooking for tough cuts of meat            e.   pan broil

2.053   _____   dry heat cooking, reserved for most tender cuts                f.   braising


**Match the cookies** (each answer, 2 point).

2.054   _____   formed into small balls and flattened with a fork              a.   drop

2.055   _____   stiff dough that is cut into fancy shapes                       b.   refrigerator

2.056   _____   rich in shortening and sugar—chilled                           c.   molded

2.057   _____   baked as a sheet in a shallow pan                              d.   rolled

2.058   _____   soft batter consistency—chocolate chip, for example           e.   bar

2.059   _____   soft dough squeezed out of cookie press to form fancy shapes   f.   pressed


<table>
<tr><td>79</td></tr>
<tr><td>99</td></tr>
</table>

Score   _____

Adult  Check   _____

Initial          Date

50

# III. MEAL PLANNING

Meal planning becomes a joy, not a chore, when you know food well enough to plan so that your meals are special—especially good, nourishing, satisfying, delightful to eat. Then they will also be a pleasure to prepare. You will have the opportunity to enjoy the results three times a day, 1,095 meals a year. Meal planning includes menus, grocery lists, and grocery shopping. You will be given the opportunity to demonstrate your skills in each of these areas.

## SECTION OBJECTIVES

**Review these objectives.** When you have completed this section, you should be able to:

6.  Demonstrate skill in planning menus.

7.  Demonstrate skill in making a grocery list and purchasing the groceries.

## MENUS

Knowing the nutritive value of foods is a valuable tool for creating healthy menus for your family. The pamphlet, *Nutritive Value of Foods* was provided for you with your Family and Consumer Science LIFEPACs. Become familiar with its use. When you prepare your menus for a week, in Exercise 3.5 you will want to refer to this pamphlet to make sure you are planning nutritious, well-balanced meals.

**Complete the following activity.**

3.1 Below is a chart with various foods listed in the left column. Use the pamphlet *Nutritive Value of Foods* to complete the chart.

| FOOD | AMOUNT | CALORIE | PROTEIN grams | FAT grams | CARBO-HYDRATES grams | CALCIUM milligrams | IRON milligrams |
|------|--------|---------|---------------|-----------|---------------------|--------------------|-----------------|
| Margarine | 1 Tbsp | | | | | | |
| Cheddar cheese | 1 Ounce | | | | | | |
| Whole milk | 1 Cup | | | | | | |
| Egg | 1 fried in margarine | | | | | | |
| Apple | 1 | | | | | | |
| Banana | 1 | | | | | | |
| Peach | 1 | | | | | | |

51

| FOOD | AMOUNT | CALORIE | PROTEIN grams | FAT grams | CARBO-HYDRATES grams | CALCIUM milligrams | IRON milligrams |
|---|---|---|---|---|---|---|---|
| Bagel | 1 | | | | | | |
| Bread | 1 slice | | | | | | |
| Fruit Loops | 1 ounce | | | | | | |
| Angel food cake | 1 Piece | | | | | | |
| Cake | | | | | | | |
| Oatmeal | 1 Cup | | | | | | |
| Chocolate chip cookie | 1 | | | | | | |
| White rice | 1 Cup | | | | | | |
| Peanut butter | 1 Tbsp | | | | | | |
| Sirloin steak | 3 ounces | | | | | | |
| Bacon | 3 med. slices | | | | | | |
| Canadian bacon | 2 slices | | | | | | |
| Cheese pizza | 1 slice | | | | | | |
| Chicken drumstick | 1 | | | | | | |
| Tomato soup | 1 Cup | | | | | | |
| Asparagus | 1 Cup | | | | | | |
| Carrot | 1 | | | | | | |
| Baked potato with skin | 1 medium | | | | | | |

| FOOD | AMOUNT | POTASSIUM | SODIUM | VIT. A INTL-UNITS | THIAMIN- | RIBO-FLAVIN | NIACIN |
|---|---|---|---|---|---|---|---|
| Margarine | 1 Tbsp | | | | | | |
| Cheddar cheese | 1 Ounce | | | | | | |
| Whole Milk | 1 Cup | | | | | | |
| Egg | 1 fried in margarine | | | | | | |
| Apple | 1 | | | | | | |
| Banana | 1 | | | | | | |
| Peach | 1 | | | | | | |
| Bagel | 1 | | | | | | |
| Bread | 1 slice | | | | | | |
| Fruit Loops | 1 ounce | | | | | | |
| Angel food cake | 1 Piece | | | | | | |
| Cake | | | | | | | |
| Oatmeal | 1 Cup | | | | | | |

| FOOD | AMOUNT | POTASSIUM | SODIUM | VIT. A INTL-UNITS | THIAMIN- | RIBO-FLAVIN | NIACIN |
|---|---|---|---|---|---|---|---|
| Chocolate chip cookie | 1 | | | | | | |
| White rice | 1 Cup | | | | | | |
| Peanut butter | 1 Tbsp | | | | | | |
| Sirloin steak | 3 ounces | | | | | | |
| Bacon | 3 med. slices | | | | | | |
| Canadian bacon | 2 slices | | | | | | |
| Cheese pizza | 1 slice | | | | | | |
| Chicken drumstick | 1 | | | | | | |
| Tomato soup | 1 Cup | | | | | | |
| Asparagus | 1 Cup | | | | | | |
| Carrot | 1 | | | | | | |
| Baked potato with skin | 1 medium | | | | | | |

(The figures in the above chart may differ depending on the edition of *Nutritive Value of Foods* used.)

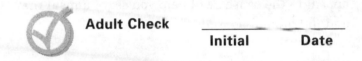

**Adult Check**

_____
Initial          Date

Great meals are satisfying in many ways. They satisfy nutritionally by including foods from MyPlate. These meals should be visually appealing as well as pleasing to the palettes of family members, with contrasts of color, form, and texture. It is important to serve hot foods hot and cold foods cold.

There are four easy ways to simplify your designs for meals.

1. Usually choose your main dish first, making this a good protein source. Then, fill in with other foods designed to supplement the main dish.

2. Be sure that the menu you plan will be appetizing with contrasts in color, texture, and flavor. For instance, if your meal includes the red of meat and the yellow, green, and white of vegetables and fruit, it is likely to be nutritionally balanced, as well as attractive and appealing.

3. Does the menu seem right for the season of the year? You want something hot and hearty after winter sports or cool and light on a hot summer day. Take advantage of seasonal specialties to add variety to good menus. Check coupons and newspapers for store specials, especially for the main dishes. Complimentary foods are fairly easy to substitute once you are at the store.

4. Remember the needs and appetites of those for whom you are preparing the meal. By all means introduce new foods and dishes, but couple them with old-time favorites.

The average family meal consists of three courses: appetizer, the main course and the dessert. The appetizer stimulates and provokes the appetite. Juice is a good appetizer for breakfast; fruit, salad, and soup are good appetizers for lunch and dinner. The main course is the major theme and the heartiest part of the meal, along with its accompaniments. The dessert is the grand finale and can help round out the meal and help balance it nutritionally in flavor, color, and texture. Not all meals will have all three courses and some will have more. The key is to make variety your rule.

Cooking is an art that appeals to the five senses. There are really only four types of taste: sweet, sour, salty, and bitter. Try to incorporate at least two or three of each of these into every meal. Of course, it is important to appeal to the sense of smell. The aroma wafting from the kitchen can either draw your family into the kitchen or repel them. Food needs to smell appealing —not burned or sour. Sound is another crowd-drawing sense. Bacon frying and popcorn popping are two attention-getters. The sense of touch can be satisfied with the different textures of food. For example, pudding should be soft-as-silk and smooth, whereas cereals and celery need to be crisp and crunchy. Last but not least is the sense of sight. The food you serve should be appealing to the eye. Serve a variety of colors so that the plate of food is attractive and colorful. For example, macaroni and cheese, corn and pineapple slices make a very dull-looking plate of food—all yellows and oranges. However, macaroni and cheese, green beans and cranberry sauce gives not only variety in color but also variety in taste and texture. Remembering to appeal to the senses will help you serve a meal that is appetizing and nutritional as well.

**A well-prepared meal appeals to all of the senses.**

---

**Answer the following questions.**

3.2    The four easy ways of simplifying your menu design are as follows.

    a.  Choose your _____ first.

    b.  Be sure your menu is appetizing with contrasts in _____ , _____ , and _____ .

    c.  The menu should be appropriate for the _____ of the year.

    d.  Remember the _____ and _____ for whom you are preparing the meal.

3.3    List the three courses of an average family meal.

    a.  _____

    b.  _____

    c.  _____

3.4    Cooking is an art that appeals to the five senses. Explain. _____
_____
_____

**Complete the following activity.**

3.5 Make up a week's (seven days) menus for all three meals. Remember to keep nutrients, calories, and variety in mind. Use the chart below.

| DAY | BREAKFAST | LUNCH | DINNER |
|---|---|---|---|
| Sunday | | | |
| Monday | | | |
| Tuesday | | | |
| Wednesday | | | |
| Thursday | | | |
| Friday | | | |
| Saturday | | | |

 **Adult Check**

_____

Initial      Date

## MAKING A GROCERY LIST

Now that you have planned your meals for the week, you are ready to make a list of the ingredients and foods you will need. Be sure to use the *Nutritive Value of Foods* as a guide for including the nutrients needed for well-balanced, nutritional meals. Include the number of calories.

Organize your list into food groups or into categories according to how your grocery store is arranged. For example, you might want to use the following food groups: produce, dairy products, bakery purchases, meats, canned goods, fresh fruits and vegetables, baking needs, cereals, and frozen foods. You will have to come up with a system that best fits your needs. It is worth the extra effort at home and will save you many steps and retracing of steps at the grocery store. Stay within your set budget.

After making your list, double check to make sure you have everything you need and that you have correctly estimated prices to stay within your budget. You will want to organize your coupons as well. Take only those you are sure you will need according to your list or you will find yourself buying items that are not on your list. Be prepared to make substitutions if prices of certain items do not match your estimated cost or if the item you want to purchase is not available.

When you arrive at the store, stay focused on the task at hand. Remember, it is the goal of the store to sell you as much of whatever they can. Store specials and sales do not always make the best purchases. There is a good chance these items may go to waste because you do not have them planned in your menus. Stick to your list whenever possible. Do not forget to read labels for nutritional value, ingredients, serving portions, and cost per unit. You may want to substitute a store brand for a name brand or a sale item.

**Stick to your list!**

---

**Complete the following activities.**

3.6    Make a grocery list from the menus you planned in activity 3.5. You may assume that you already have staples such as flour, sugar, and seasonings, but you should plan on buying eggs, milk, bread, butter, etc.

| | | |
|---|---|---|
| _____ | _____ | _____ |
| _____ | _____ | _____ |
| _____ | _____ | _____ |
| _____ | _____ | _____ |
| _____ | _____ | _____ |

3.7    **Grocery Shopping:** Go to the supermarket and write down prices for each item on your list. Indicate if you had a manufacturer's coupon, a store coupon or store discount. What was your budget amount? How much did you spend? How much under or over was your total?

**Adult Check**  _____

                  **Initial        Date**

    Review the material in this section in preparation for the Self Test. This Self Test will check your mastery of this particular section as well as your knowledge of the previous sections.

# SELF TEST 3

**Fill in the blanks** (each answer, 2 points).

3.01    When designing your menu the _____ should be chosen first. It should be a good source of _____ .

3.02    Your menu should have contrasts in color, _____ and _____ .

3.03    Your menu should be appropriate for the _____ of the year.

3.04    Remember the _____ and _____ for those you are cooking.

3.05    The three courses that an average family meal consists of are _____ , _____ , and _____ .

**Answer** *true* **or** *false* (each answer, 1 point).

3.06    _____    The most important characteristic of prepared cereal is crispness.

3.07    _____    Amino acids are chemicals or building blocks used to make proteins.

3.08    _____    Starches are simple carbohydrates.

3.09    _____    Vitamin D is the "sunshine" vitamin.

3.010   _____    Vitamin B helps promote proper digestion.

3.011   _____    Vitamin K is important for vision.

3.012   _____    Children should begin using the Dietary Guidelines for Americans and MyPlate at the age of 3.

3.013   _____    Vegetables grown underground should be cooked in a covered pan.

3.014   _____    Yeast is responsible for elasticity and extensibility in bread dough.

3.015   _____    The character of cheese depends on its age as well as its variety.

3.016   _____    A carrot is an example of a root vegetable.

**Complete the following with a short answer** (5 points).

3.017   Cooking is an art that appeals to the five senses. Explain. _____

_____

_____

_____

# IV. FOOD SERVICE

The term *table service* refers to the way or manner in which the foods are served at the table. There are two types of table service: informal and formal. The informal type of meal service includes four styles: blue-plate, family style, buffet, and compromise. The formal styles are English and Russian. This section of LIFEPAC 3 will explain each of these styles in more detail. Learning to properly set the table and to wait the table will also be covered. It is an embarrassing experience to be at a formal affair and not know how to use all the knives, forks, and spoons. You shall learn the appropriate use and order for each item of the table setting. How fun it is to be the one who can easily guide others at the table, in the proper usage of the silverware, glasses, plates.

## SECTION OBJECTIVES

**Review these objectives.** When you have completed this section, you should be able to:

10. Identify the different types of table service.

11. Demonstrate skill in table setting and table waiting.

## STYLES OF TABLE SERVICE

How do you determine which table service style to use? Breakfast and lunch are usually rushed meals, so you want to pick a quick style of service such as blue plate, buffet or family style. Dinners and special occasions are usually more formal and allow you more time, so English or Russian would make better choices.

Be careful to consider your menu when selecting a style. Simple menus are usually served simply and casually. Elaborate menus are served more formally. Consider the dining space, available table appointments, time available for serving and eating a meal, number of people, and the occasion. Let's take a closer look at the different styles.

The *blue plate* style is where food is placed on individual plates in the kitchen and brought to the table at each **cover**. The advantages of this style are: the plate service is quick, you don't have any serving dishes to wash and it is a good service for small tables or rooms with not much space (apartments). There are two obvious disadvantages of the blue plate style of service: it is not a good service for a large group of people and guests will feel obligated to eat everything on their plate.

Your menu for the blue plate style of service should include foods that are easy to serve on individual plates and food that is suitable to be served at the last minute. Examples of suitable types of food are spaghetti, ice cream or crepes.

The *buffet style* of service is where food is arranged on a table and the guests walk by, help themselves to the food and then find a seat. It is the best way to serve a large number of guests. It is easy to set up and a nice way to display food items. Another advantage is that it is informal and develops a friendly atmosphere. There are some disadvantages to this style of service as well. Service can be slow and the food may not keep the desired temperature without proper equipment. Also adequate seating arrangements may be a problem.

You should never serve more than two courses buffet style. Never serve the main dish and the dessert courses at the same time. The food should appear in decreasing order of importance: main dish, vegetables, salads, breads, beverage. Accompaniments should be on the table by the item they accompany. For example, salad dressing, and croutons should be located by the salads. Plates should be at the beginning of the table and flatware and napkins should be at the end of the table.

After the guests serve themselves from the buffet table, they may be seated at tables such as card tables, or individual snack tables. If tables are not available, they may eat from trays or plates, lap-style.

When using the *family style*, serving dishes are placed on the table with the serving utensil beside them. The dishes are passed around the table and each person serves himself. This is an easy and fast way to serve people. Everyone can select what they want and how much they want. It also is a good way of starting conversation as you pass the bowls around the table. You can serve anything that is easy to serve from a bowl or platter. The main disadvantage of this style is there are more dishes to wash.

Never start the meal with the utensil in the serving dish; it should always be beside the dish. When placing utensils with the serving bowls, make sure the utensil to be used with the bowl is placed facing someone, so that person will know to start that dish. Set the individual plates at each cover and the serving dishes on the table before the meal is announced.

The *English style* is more formal. The food is served in courses by a waitress. Courses are served onto plates by the host and hostess and the waitress takes the plate to the guests. This gives special attention to each guest and gives opportunity for conversation at the table while the food is being served. It also makes a nice display of food.

Some of the disadvantages are: there are more dishes to wash and it takes longer to serve the food and, therefore, longer to eat. It is a very detailed service and can be embarrassing if you do not do it correctly. You should serve food that is easy to dish up and place on plates.

You must have two courses for it to be called English. The soup or salad course is served by the hostess, the main course is served by the host and the dessert course is served by the hostess.

The *compromise style* of table service is a combination of English and another service, usually the blue plate. The first course is served English style and the second course is served another style. The advantage of this style of service is it gives a formal feel to the meal, yet it is a quicker form of service. However, there are more dishes and it still takes a long time.

The *Russian style* is the most dignified and elaborate style of service. All the food is served from the kitchen by a waitress or waiter. The food is served on individual plates or the guests may serve themselves as the waiter holds the dish. It is very formal and elegant. It is a nice service to try a variety of garnishing. Of course, there are lots and lots of dishes and it takes a very long time, usually one and a half to two hours.

The menu requires seven courses: appetizer, soup, fish, meat or main dish, salad, dessert, and **demitasse** which is strong coffee, mints, and nuts. Course portions are small—as light as possible. Each item should be well seasoned and garnished. Each course should have some kind of bread accompaniment. Water is the only beverage served.

The table is set with a white tablecloth, white napkins, and white candles. There is no centerpiece and no salt and pepper shakers. Each cover is set with flatware up to the dessert course. A **service plate** (a very decorative, large plate) is used at each cover. A different service plate may be used at each cover. No food is placed directly onto the service plate. Service plates remain at the cover through the third course. Each course preceding the main course is served on a **liner plate**.

Finger bowls (bowls with warm soapy water) are used between the sixth and seventh course. You dip your fingers in the bowl to clean them. Demitasse is served in the family or living room.

Whatever style of service you choose, remember variety is once again the rule. You can have fun trying each new style.

**Answer the following questions.**

4.1 What is meant by the term *table service*? _____

4.2 What are the two types of services? a. _____ b. _____

4.3 Breakfast would usually be an example of which type of table service? _____

4.4 What are the three informal styles of table service given in the reading?

a. _____ b. _____ c. _____

4.5 What are the two formal styles of table service given above? a. _____ b. _____

4.6 What are some things to consider when deciding what style of table service to use?

_____

_____

4.7 Which style of table service involves serving food on individual plates filled in the kitchen, and brought to the table at each cover? _____

4.8 Which style of table service is best for a large crowd because guests serve themselves?

_____

4.9 How is the food set up on a buffet table? _____

4.10 Which style of table service is the most relaxing and friendly because food is passed around the table and everyone serves himself? _____

4.11 Which formal style of table service is the most elaborate? _____

4.12 Who puts the dessert on the plates before they are served to the guest in an English style service? _____

4.13 Define the following words.

a. cover _____

b. compromise style _____

4.14 List the seven courses of the Russian style of table service.

a. _____

b. _____

c. _____

d. _____

e. _____

f. _____

g. _____

## TABLE SETTING

The appearance of the table and the food can stimulate your appetite and mealtime enjoyment. An attractively set table helps to create the mood for enjoying good food and pleasant conversation. When you plan the setting for a meal, consider what is appropriate and which items look nice together. Your choice

Dessert Fork
Butter Knife
Bread Plate
Dinner Plate
Dinner Fork
Salad Fork
Napkin

Water Glass
Beverage Glass
Dessert Spoon
Dinner Knife
Spoon
Soup Spoon

of color and pattern or design in table appointments can contribute to the beauty of your table. A well-set table is essential for an attractively served meal.

It is perfectly appropriate to mix sets of dishes as long as they share roughly the same weight and feel. Begin your setting with dinner plates or larger decorative plate liners. Arrange no more than three pieces of silverware on each side of the dinner plate. The service should be placed in the order of use for each course, beginning on the outside and working in. Forks go on the left, knives and spoons on the right. Knives always should be placed with the cutting edge toward the dinner plate.

Place dessert forks and spoons just above the dinner plate; the spoon closest to the plate with the handle facing right and the fork above the spoon with the handle facing left.

Set glasses to the right, above the knife, beginning with a water goblet, followed by the beverage glass. If a hot beverage is the only beverage served, the cup and saucer are placed in the water glass position at the tip of the knife. The handle of the cup should be directed to the right.

Place the bread plate level with the glasses on the left hand side, above the forks. A butter knife should be placed along the top of the plate with the handle facing right. If a salad plate is set, put it slightly to the side and level with the top of the forks on the left. Place the napkins to the left of the forks with the openings facing away from the flatware, or on the center of the dinner plate or liner if the first course will be served after everyone is seated.

Appetizers, soups or desserts in their bowls or on their plates should always be placed on a large plate or liner, which is removed along with the empty dish.

Now that the basic table is all set, decide where you will place bread baskets, salt and pepper, butter dishes, and any other essentials.

A centerpiece adds beauty and gives color to your table setting. It is often placed near the center of the table, but may be placed at the side or end of the table when convenient. The centerpiece should harmonize in color with the room, food, and dishes. It should be low enough (about 10 inches high) so that you can see each other across the table. Flowers, plants, fruits, fresh vegetables, ornamental glass, pottery, and other household items are often used.

**Answer the following questions.**

4.15 Can you mix sets of dishes? _____

4.16 How many pieces of silverware are allowed on each side of the dinner plate? _____

4.17 What is the important rule to remember when placing knives? _____

4.18 Where do dessert forks and spoons belong? _____

4.19 Where does the bread plate belong? _____

4.20 How do you arrange the beverage glasses? _____.

4.21 Why use a centerpiece? _____

**Complete the following activity.**

4.22 Practice setting a proper table setting for one person.

Adult Check _____

Initial          Date

---

## TABLE WAITING

It is important to have an understanding of proper table waiting. You have spent a lot of time preparing a special meal for a special occasion; it would be a shame to spoil the effect by improper service or table waiting.

When you bring your guests into the room, the candles should be lit, and the water glasses filled. Don't wait for people to ask for water. Nowadays it is almost impolite not to serve a glass of water.

There is less confusion if you have **placecards** already positioned so your guests will easily see where they have been assigned to sit. It is your responsibility to carefully think through the most comfortable arrangement for all guests' enjoyment of the evening.

In the family style of service, food moves toward the right around the table. The only exception is when someone asks for a particular dish and it is much closer to pass it to the left rather than to the right.

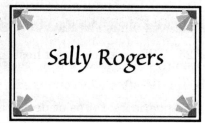

Sally Rogers

**Placecards minimize confusion for guests.**

There are some specific rules to follow when waiting a table. At a meal with both host and hostess, serve the person seated to the right of the host first. At a meal with a hostess only, serve the person seated to her right first. Proceed around the table counterclockwise (left to right). Once the order has been established, be consistent with it throughout the meal for all serving and clearing. The only exception to this is during a course served at the table by the hostess. During that course, all serving and clearing should begin with the person seated to her right, even if the person to the host's right is served first during the rest of the meal.

Which hand? Which side? The rule is, serve from the left and clear from the right. This means that you place a plate in front of the person with your left hand coming in on their left side. You then remove a plate with your right hand coming in on their right side.

Beverages should be refilled throughout a meal as needed. Replenish when the glasses are down to about 1/4 full. Fill the glass to 1/2–1 inch from the rim. Because beverage glasses are on the right side of the cover, it is best to reach in with left or right hand and remove from the table on the right side of the person. Hold it behind the person and refill the beverage with the pitcher held in the opposite hand. Replace the glass. If you need to re-ice the beverage glasses, do so for all diners before replenishing the beverage. Stand to the right of the person, hold the bowl of ice in the left hand, tongs in the right hand. Reach in with tongs and place ice cubes in the glass. Complete the replenishing of one beverage before beginning the second beverage.

Once the last course before dessert is finished, clear the table of breads, butters, salt, pepper, and remaining condiments.

Serve dessert according to the style of the meal service. For example: for the blue plate style service, approach the table with two filled dessert plates. Serve the one in the left hand to the first person on his left side. Transfer the dessert plate in the right hand to the left hand to serve the second person. Repeat until all are served.

It is often fun to move the dessert or the demitasse to another room for variety and conversation. This also allows a guest to mingle and talk with someone other than his or her table partner. This dessert or demitasse can be served buffet style or by having waiters serve. When you serve the demitasse, it is nice to serve nuts and mints as well.

If these directions seem somewhat confusing, then go back and walk through the directions as you read them again. Practice.

---

**Answer the following questions.**

4.23   What is a placecard? _____

4.24   In what direction do you pass food around the table?_____

4.25   When there are a host and a hostess, which person at the table is served first?_____

4.26   Do you serve clockwise or counterclockwise?_____

4.27   The rule is serve from the _____ and clear from the _____ .

4.28   How full should beverage glasses be filled? _____

4.29   When do you clear off breads, salt, pepper, and condiments?_____

**Complete the following activity.**

4.30   Demonstrate your ability to wait a table. Serve the main course, beverages and desserts for both the informal style and the formal style of service.

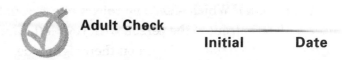

Adult Check _____

Initial          Date

63

Complete the following Family and Consumer Science LIFEPAC 2 and LIFEPAC 3 Cumulative Activity.

4.31 Prepare three meals; breakfast, lunch, and dinner. Give the menus, the ingredients, the nutritional values of each item on the menu, the total calorie count, and the serving style. Have your parent or teacher fill out the following grade sheet for each meal.

| Menu | Ingredients | Nutritional value | Calorie count | Serving style |
|------|-------------|-------------------|---------------|---------------|
| Breakfast | | | | |
| Lunch | | | | |
| Dinner | | | | |

Adult Check _____

Initial     Date

| Grading Specifications and number of points possible for each meal. | Points earned Breakfast | Points earned Lunch | Points earned Dinner |
|---|---|---|---|
| Appearance of the food<br>Colorful, pleasing to the eye, appealing<br>10 points | | | |
| Garnish.<br>Did the student use garnish appropriately?<br>5 points | | | |
| Temperature of the food.<br>Was the food served at the proper temperature?<br>(Hot or cold)<br>5 points | | | |
| Flavor of the food.<br>Was the food good? (Be honest)<br>10 points | | | |
| Was the meal nutritional and well-balanced?<br>10 points | | | |
| Was the meal served on time?<br>5 points | | | |
| Food Service.<br>Was the table setting and the service style compatible with the menu?<br>5 points | | | |
| Total points _____ | | | |

**Adult Check**    _____

Initial        Date

. . . . . . . . . . . . . . . . . . . . . . . . . . . . . . . . . . . . . . . . . . . . . . . . . . . . . . . .

Before you take this last Self Test, you may want to do one or more of these self checks.

1. _____ Read the objectives. Determine if you can do them.

2. _____ Restudy the material related to any objectives that you cannot do.

3. _____ Use the SQ3R study procedure to review the material:
   a. **S**can the sections.
   b. **Q**uestion yourself again.
   c. **R**ead to answer your questions.
   d. **R**ecite the answers to yourself.
   e. **R**eview areas you didn't understand.

4. _____ Review all vocabulary, activities, and Self Tests, writing a correct answer for each wrong answer.

# SELF TEST 4

**Fill in the blanks** (each answer, 3 points).

4.01    The two types of table service are _____ and _____ .

4.02    The two formal styles of table service are _____ and _____ .

4.03    Two things to consider when deciding what style of table service to use are _____ and _____ .

**Choose the correct answer** (each answer, 2 points).

4.04    Food moves toward the ( right / left ) around the table.

4.05    Serve the person seated to the ( right / left ) of the host first.

4.06    Serve ( clockwise / counterclockwise ).

4.07    Serve from the ( right / left ) and clear from the ( right / left ).

**Matching** (each answer, 2 points).

4.08    _____    plates filled by hostess, then served in courses by a waitress        a.  blue plate

4.09    _____    best for large groups because guests serve themselves              b   buffet

4.010   _____    food is passed around the table and everyone serves himself        c.  family

4.011   _____    most elaborate style with seven courses                            d.  compromise

4.012   _____    individual plates are filled in the kitchen and brought to the      e.  English
                     table at each cover
                                                                                        f.  Russian
4.013   _____    combination of English and one other style of service

**Define the following words** (each answer, 2 points).

4.014   Demitasse _____

        _____

4.015   Table Service _____

        _____

4.016   Cover _____

        _____

**Answer** *true* **or** *false* (each answer, 2 points).

4.017   _____    Fiber is a plant material humans cannot digest.

4.018   _____    Vitamin C helps keep teeth and gums healthy.

4.019   _____    The function of iron is to help regulate thyroid activity.

66

4.020 _____ The average adult needs 2–4 servings of vegetables a day.

4.021 _____ Fruit is the best source of vitamins.

4.022 _____ Milk is the best source of protein.

4.023 _____ Anorexia nervosa is generally a problem found in young girls.

4.024 _____ Diabetes is caused by an abnormal glucose level.

4.025 _____ Cheese should be cooked at a high temperature for a very short time.

4.026 _____ Air is the leavening agent for an angel food cake.

4.027 _____ Bisque is a clear soup made from beef stock.

4.028 _____ Bananas are grown on trees.

4.029 _____ Rolled cookies are cut into fancy shapes.

4.030 _____ Choosing the main dish is the first step in designing a menu.

4.031 _____ Cooking is an art that should appeal to the five senses.

**Complete the drawing and label** (each answer 2 points).

4.032   Draw and label a proper place setting. It should include a dinner plate, bread plate with knife, dinner knife, spoon, soup spoon, dinner fork, salad fork, dessert fork and spoon, napkin, water glass, beverage glass.

Score _____

Adult Check _____
Initial    Date

67

# GLOSSARY

**anemia.** Deficiency of the hemoglobin, often accompanied by a reduced number of red blood cells and causing pallor, weakness, and breathlessness.

**carotene.** Any of three isometric red hydrocarbons found in many plants, especially carrots and transformed into vitamin A in the liver.

**constipation.** A condition of the bowels in which the feces are dry and hardened and evacuation is difficult and infrequent.

**cover.** Each person's place setting, including all the table appointments he or she will need for the meal.

**demitasse.** A small cup of strong, dark coffee served after dinner.

**dietitian.** A person who is an expert on nutrition and dietetics.

**elasticity.** The property of a substance that enables it to change its length, volume, or shape in direct response to a force and to recover its original form upon the removal of the force; flexibility, resilience.

**extensibility.** The property of a substance that enables it to be stretched out.

**goiter.** Enlargement of the thyroid gland on the front and sides of the neck.

**liner plate.** The plate that sits between the service plate and the plate that has the food on it.

**marinade.** A seasoned liquid in which meat, fish, vegetables are steeped before cooking.

**metabolism.** The sum of the physical and chemical processes in the body.

**osteoporosis.** A bone disorder marked by a decrease in bone mass; can cause fractures and back pain.

**palatable.** Pleasing or acceptable to the taste.

**placecard.** An individual card placed at each cover with the guest's name on it, indicating where he/she is to sit.

**popovers.** A puffed muffin with a hollow center.

**scones.** Flat, round, leavened cakes made of oatmeal, wheat flour, barley meal or the like.

**sedentary.** Accustomed to sit or rest a great deal or to take little exercise.

**service plate.** A decorative plate that is set at each cover. No food is put directly on this plate. It remains at the cover through the third course.

**translucency (translucent).** Permitting light to pass through but diffusing it so that objects on the other side are not clearly visible.

# BIBLIOGRAPHY

Arkin, Frieda, *Kitchen Wisdom*, Budget Book Service, Inc., NY, 1993.

*Betty Crocker's New Cookbook*, Macmillan, NY, eighth edition, 1998.

Rosso, Julee and Lukin, Sheila, *The New Basic Cookbook*, Workman Publishing, NY, 1989.

Wessinger, Joanna, *The Home Answer Book*, Harper Collins Publishers, NY, 1995.

Before taking the LIFEPAC Test, you may want to do one or more of these self checks.

1. _____ Read the objectives. Check to see if you can do them.
2. _____ Restudy the material related to any objectives that you cannot do.
3. _____ Use the SQ3R study procedure to review the material.
4. _____ Review activities, Self Tests, and LIFEPAC vocabulary words.
5. _____ Restudy areas of weakness indicated by the last Self Test.